Dream Catcher

POETRY EDITORS
PETER LEWIN
JENNY CLARKSON

FICTION EDITOR
CHRIS FIRTH

CO-ORDINATOR
JOE WARNER

GENERAL EDITOR
PAUL SUTHERLAND

VISUAL ARTS EDITOR
HEATHER HARKER

CONSULTANT EDITOR
IAN PARKS

CONSULTANT EDITOR
(NEW ZEALAND)
JENNY ARGANTE

CONSULTANT EDITOR
FOR NEW ZEALAND FICTION
MORAG MCGILL

Introduction

Welcome to *Dream Catcher* issue 12, and a special welcome to New Zealand contributors.

From *Dream Catcher's* beginning, I have encouraged a democratic approach making the magazine available to many contributors with the aim of giving our readership diversity and excellence. Issue 12 is the first time we have extended these objectives to almost half the publication being used by a special interest group, in this case from a specific location, New Zealand. In years ahead, we hope to alternate specific and generic issues, though this prospect requires that each project be workable.

This New Zealand issue has been tenable due to the input of Jenny Argante who has become a co-editor. Known more as Jenny Brice to a British readers, she moved to the southern hemisphere three years ago and has sustained contact with *Dream Catcher* proposing and showing the value of a New Zealand orientated issue. She has acted as a conduit, collecting and passing on submissions and raising funds. Thank you to the Wellington Arts Initiative for their support. Jenny has kept in touch till the project's completion, guiding some of New Zealand's best known poets and short story writers toward *Dream Catcher*, promoting the journal in her new homeland.

I recognise giving half to New Zealand authors severely reduces the space for British writers from whom the vast majority of submissions come and who represent by far our largest audience. I hope British readers accept that the periodic concentration on a topic or location enriches and deepens the writing published and opens-up new markets and readerships to Dream Catcher's long term benefit.

In her Foreword Jenny discusses the transformation she experienced on coming to New Zealand, its revitalising effect on her creative life. I encountered a similar transition disembarking at Tilbury thirty years ago: old historiated Britain became to my eyes a new and unknown territory to explore. More or less my excitement has been maintained through years of content and discontent. In this issue many authors express our common legacy of belonging to a place and our recurrent rootlessness. At times these themes are shown as in conflict, sometimes as converging identities or as vital elements in the mix of self-metamorphosis.

Paul Sutherland

Foreword

When I came to New Zealand three years ago, not entirely by design, I bought the local paper and began to read the literature of the country.

I did this successfully enough to come 3rd in a Takahe competition with an essay on 'Reading the Past, Writing the Future'. I'm now embarked on an writing course to learn to 'write Kiwi'. I don't know exactly what I mean by that, but I see it as something different from writing Pom.

Our two countries share a language – though New Zealanders also have Te Reo and the Maori oral tradition to call upon. We share that multiculturalism that in any nation assists the arts to grow, evolve and change. Share some common history.

Yet here there is something unique that crept into being when Jane Mander threw off the mantle of colonialism with her Story of a 'New Zealand River'. In latter years *Once Were Warriors* – film and book – made Alan Duff internationally known alongside others such as Janet Frame, Katherine Mansfield, James Baxter, Keri Hulme and C.K. Stead. *Poetry New Zealand* sells substantially in America as a text in creative writing classes. Poetry overall has its own mannerisms and intellectual tradition. New Zealand writers sell steadily not only at home and in Australia but also in the UK, USA and the Pacific. Literary journals of all kinds abound – *Landfall, Southern Ocean Review, Spin, Takahe, Trout* and *JAAM*. Creative writing courses like that run by exemplar Bill Manhire flourish and expand not only in Wellington but beyond.

I've been on a 3-year voyage of discovery, and it's been illuminating. What Paul and I are sharing with you in this edition of *Dream Catcher* is only a minute portion of what's on offer. So read on beyond the covers.

Literature is the key to other classes, other codes and other cultures. On the map, New Zealand is a small country many, many miles away. Here I have struck gold. As I said in my own poem on 'Coming to New Zealand':

> Perhaps I had to cross the continents
> to find a different self, wary and bold,
> like these electric skies,
> abundant, elastic.

New Zealand writers, both Maori and Pakeha, have given me the chance to explore many different selves, not only my own. What else can I say but Thank you?

Jenny Argante

Contents - Authors

Introduction	II
Foreword	III
Photography, Sue Stockwell	1
Hurricanes/Wild Water *by Alistair Paterson*	3
Historia Calamitatum *by Alistair Paterson*	4
New Zealand *by Alistair Paterson*	6
From The 1875 - Shippings Arrival File *by Elizabeth Smither*	9
Kool Notes For You *by Mark Pirie*	10
Riverton Beach Poem For Tim *by Mark Pirie*	11
Two National Myths For M.H. Holcroft *by Mark Pirie*	12
No Ordinary Son Hone Tuwhare Goes North *by Denis Welch*	14
Canterbury Gold *by Kay McGregor*	21
The Empty Dovecote *by Catherine Mair & Patricia Prime*	22
The Tent Factory *by Tim Upperton*	24
How To Talk To A Peacock *by James Norcliffe*	27
Tchaikovsky Enters A New And Darker Period Of His Life *by James Norcliffe*	28
Antigone In The Hot Pool *by James Norcliffe*	29
Nuclear Free *by Tim O'Brien*	30
Urupa *by Michael Lee*	35
Cat And Mouse *by Sue Emms*	37
The World Head Quarters Of The Verb: The Wellington Writers' Walk *by Peter Farrell*	42
Living Here *by Cilla McQueen*	48
Mining *by Owen Bullock*	50
Shark Callers *by Jennifer Compton*	52
The Weight Of Cows *by Mandy Coe*	54
The Chocolate Polisher *by Mandy Coe*	55
Doulton Lady *by Jill Eulalie Dawson*	56
Alchemy *by Char March*	57

Contents - Authors

City Of Strangers *by David Ford*	58
Echoes *by Idris Caffrey*	59
Matterhorn *by Lotte Kramer*	60
Boy: *by Lotte Kramer*	61
Nigeria High Commission *by Ugbana Oyet*	62
My Friend Est *by Ugbana Oyet*	64
Duncan's Dream *by Mandy MacFarlane*	65
F817GFE *by Sam Gardiner*	69
Dear You *by Sam Gardiner*	70
None Of His Own *by Sam Gardiner*	71
The New Kimono *by Gloria Grove-Stephenson*	72
Suddenly Street Lights For Eleanor Wilner *by Lucy Brennan*	73
September Dying *by Lucy Brennan*	74
The Audition *by Elizabeth Stott*	75
The Sand-Timer *by R. J. Stallon*	75
Nymphomaniac *by Mark Czanik*	76
Witness *by André Mangeot*	78
After Eight *by Emma-Jane Arkady*	80
After The Hurricane *by K. V. Skene*	81
Violon D' Ingres After A Photograph By Man Ray *by Kathryn Daszkiewicz*	82
Hot Love *by Kathryn Daszkiewicz*	83
Letter To Wilgefortis *by Kathryn Daszkiewicz*	84
No Demand *by Jenny Swann*	85
Thinking Of Benny *by Gordon Wardman*	86
Photos *by Julia Davis*	87
Driving Trough Jerusalem *by Ruth Beckett*	88
Impossible Lake *by Chris Firth*	90
The Sheathed Smile *by Mike Barlow*	103
Report *by Angela Rigsby*	104
Separation *by Ian Seed*	105

Contents - Authors

Corpse by *Ian Seed*	106
Dad - Not Dead by *Stephen Baker*	106
Dear Father by *Juned Subhan*	108
Water by *Joseph Allen*	109
Roads by *Gary Allen*	110
A Matter Of Time by *Edward Storey*	111
The Dead by *Mario Petrucci*	112
Shaping Destiny by *Cathy Grindrod*	114
On The Theft Of A 4,000 Year Old Fish From A Village Museum In Scotland by *Cathy Grindrod*	115
Silver Heart by *Ian Parks*	116
Dune Show by *Gordon Wilson*	117
A New Eden by *India Russell*	118
The Dinner Party by *India Russell*	119
The Lost Child by *Mary Knight*	121
Miniatures by *John Greeves*	125
Drawing Circles by *James Caruth*	126
The Performance by *Gaia Holmes*	127
Billy Moon by *Peter Lewin*	128
A God by *Davide Trame*	130
Five Notes On The Trumpet by *Stuart Flynn*	131
Girl, Interrupted At Her Music by *Erin L. Hickey*	132
In The Blood by *Joolz Denby*	133
What? by *Fatma Durmush*	134
In The Grand Hotel, Lincoln by *Rory Waterman*	135
If Only (We Could Trick Fate) by *Divya Mathur*	136
Traps by *Norman Jackson*	137
Wake Up by *J. Morris*	139
La Sainte Chapelle, Paris by *Nell Farrell*	140
Four Courses by *Pamela Lewis*	141

Contents - Authors

A God Just Under The Ground *by Fred Voss*	142
They Could Have Had PHDs Too *by Fred Voss*	144
Moving Into Our New Home *by Fred Voss*	145
Calls From Home *by Marion Ashton*	146
Break *by Natalie Ford*	147
Mr ISBN *by Michael Blackburn*	148
The Big Fight *by Dave Mason*	150
The Hole *by Dave Mason*	151
That Last Hello *by Daithidh MacEochaidh*	152
The Morning Brings *by Timothy Kaiser*	155
GLOSSARY OF MAORI AND NEW ZEALAND ENGLISH USAGE	157
SOURCES FOR MORE INFORMATION ON NEW ZEALAND WRITERS	158
REVIEWS	159
BIOGRAPHIES	168

Dream Catcher

Paul Sutherland,
7 Fairfield Street,
Lincoln, LN2 5NE
Tel. (07799897994)

Co-ordinator: Joe Warner
32 Queens Road,
Barnetby-le-Wold
North Lincolnshire, DN38 6JH
Tel. (07958805431)

© Alistair Paterson, Elizabeth Smither, Mark Pirie, Denis Welch, Kay McGregor, Catherine Mair, Patricia Prime, Tim Upperton, James Norcliffe, Tim O'Brien, Michael Lee, Sue Emms, Peter Farrell, Cilla McQueen, Owen Bullock, Jennifer Compton, Mandy Coe, Jill Eulalie Dawson, Char March, David Ford, Idris Caffery, Lotte Kramer, Ugbana Oyet, Mandy MacFarlane, Sam Gardiner, Gloria Grove-Stephenson, Lucy Brennan, Elizabeth Stott, R. J. Stallon, Mark Czanik, André Mangeot, Emma-Jane Arkady, K. V. Skene, Kathryn Daszkiewicz, Jenny Swann, Gordon Wardman, Julia Davis, Ruth Beckett, Chris Firth, Mike Barlow, Angela Rigsby, Ian Seed, Stephen Baker, Juned Subhan, Joseph Allen, Gary Allen, Edward Storey, Mario Perrucci, Cathy Grindrod, Ian Parks, Gordon Wilson, India Russell, Mary Knight, John Greeves, James Caruth, Gaia Holmes, Peter Lewin, Davide Trame, Stuart Flynn, Erin L. Hickey, Joolz Denby, Fatma Durmush, Rory Waterman, Divya Mathur, Norman Jackson, J. Morris, Nell Farrell, Sam Gardiner, Pamela Lewis, Fred Voss, Marion Ashton, Natalie Ford, Michael Blackburn, Dave Mason, Daithidh MacEochaidh, Timothy Kaiser, 2003

Reviewers: Morag McGill, Karen Maitland, Ian Parks, Nigel Walker

Cover Design: Steven Byford @ Properganda Design

Featured Artist: Sue Stockwell

Design and Typography by Steven Byford @ Properganda Design

The Moral Rights of the authors & artists have been asserted.

Published by Dream Catcher Books

ISSN. 1466-9455
ISBN No. 0-95450 15-0-0

The Art of Sue Stockwell

Sue Stockwell after obtaining a B.A (Hons) in Fine Art at Cumbria College of Art and Design she has taught in Workshops for adults and children using the media of print paper making and paper sculpture.

Her work is autobiographical using a small vocabulary of symbols to act out lyrical reflections on the drama of everyday life, and the emotional forces which shape them.

As a printmaker much of the imagery is developed either through the process of creating the image through etching, burnishing and scraping - repeatedly defining and erasing elements of the picture, or through the act of cutting a line into lino.

As an access into her work Sue uses the following quotation when exhibiting her work.

Sometimes............. I have caught myself in that other life, touched it, seen it to be as real as my own. From *The Passion* by Jeanette Winterson.

Photographs

Flying Not Falling	*Page 20*
Teetering On The Edge	*Page 23*
Dancing Shoes	*Page 36*
Balancing Act	*Page 51*
The Writing On The Wall	*Page 89*
Last Chick	*Page 108*
Birdsong And Rain	*Page 121*
Falling From Grace	*Page 139*

HURRICANES/ WILD WATER

It happens when the wind blows
from the north - the south -
from whatever direction
winds come from or blow to

the room suddenly cold, silent

bringing not only the welcome
& welcoming news of a lover
that she, that he's still there
they're both, however distant

covers thrown back, bed empty

close to each other & nothing's
changed, that the immutable
is truly & forever immutable -
able to withstand the howl

what might happen but shouldn't

& shriek, the ungovernable thrust
the burst of the hurricane when
it reaches the coastline, wind
& water swirl inland over towns

clothes on the floor, door open

cities, villages, country hamlets
the park across the street, the trees -
trees that have been there
a hundred years & will be there

a hundred from now ....
                it happens

Alistair Paterson

Historia Calamitatum

*tender words... and hands that sought
each other instead of books...*

                                   Pierre Abelard

1.
It's a mystery, Heloise —
where you've been
this last thousand years.
Hidden in the walls
of the Paraclete
invisible to the world?
How could the melt & lift
of hips & thighs
bring such weeping —
but of course they did
& you've been waiting
all this time, savaged
by the pangs of love
unable to escape its fetters...

2.
You wrote about it & yet
they're so little to live by
those letters — yours & his.
You kept them
(both of you kept them)
all those words, those pages
binding together two lives —
the experience of them
all that might have been
before & after merely dust
forgotten as so many lives
are forgotten because
they aren't important, don't
seem worth remembering.

3.
And if they're not worth it
-worth the remembering-
what is there that ought
to be remembered; events
& exchanges caught
like wasps in amber —
held by the intensity
of the moment: casual words
spoken by candle-light
or over dinner, the unexpected
(a glimmer of water
seen through windows)
your waiting in silence
& the dark - all those years...

Alistair Paterson

New Zealand

Contemporary poetry in New Zealand is alive and well. Undoubtedly in terms of the ever-increasing number of poets writing in this country and in the quality of their work, New Zealand is at the cutting edge of poetry development. Poets here have absorbed all the isms – from the romantics through Dadaism, modernism and postmodernism to language writing and the more extreme forms of semiotics.

Poetry in English arrived in New Zealand with the coming of the whalers and sealers who followed on the country's European rediscovery by James Cook in 1769. Whalers and sealers brought with them the shanties and songs common during this period. A few of these–including those directly connected with New Zealand, such as the anonymous ballad David Lawson–still survive. The poetry that followed the signing of the Treaty of Waitangi in February 1840, was reflective of the forms and styles then extant in England and as such was painfully unreflective of the situation the new settlers found themselves in. The largest work of the period was written by Alfred Domett (a personal friend of Robert Browning). His 'dusty epic', *Ranolf and Amohia* (1872) in twenty-five cantos, dwelt on high romance between a British adventurer and a Maori princess. Most of the poetry of the nineteenth century is stiff, stylised and now little read except for its historic value. The work of a small number of poets of the period (the late nineteenth century), such as Edward Tregear, Arthur H Adams and Blanche Baughan is still readable and genuinely reflects the New Zealand situation, as does William Pember Reeves' early environmental piece, *The Passing of the Forest*.

The first part of the twentieth century saw the development of landscape poetry, often very Wordsworthian in style. The 1920's however, saw the rise of a number of poets who for the first time broke through the colonial constraints of the nineteenth century, and began a new kind of poetry that set the scene for most of the twentieth century. They were A R D Fairburn (1904-57), R A K Mason (1905-71) and Robin Hyde (1906-39), although Hyde for the most part was not as much appreciated at the time, as she should have been. Close enough on their heels as to be virtually their contemporaries came an extremely vigorous group of poets dominated by the very English Charles Brasch (1909-73) founder of the literary journal *Landfall*, the extremely proselytizing Allen Curnow (1911-2001), and Denis Glover (1912-1980).

Throughout the 1930's these poets established a form of poetry sometimes called nationalistic which, beginning with and culminating in the publication of Allen Curnow's 1945 anthology *A Book of New Zealand Verse*, many have claimed established a watershed in this country's writing. In this respect, it threw into disrepute much of the work that had preceded it, seriously damaging the reputations of anthologists such as Quentin Pope (*Kowhai Gold*, 1930) and putting out of favour the anthologies they had compiled as it did Alexander and Currie's *A Treasury of New Zealand Verse* (1926) and *New Zealand Best Poems* (1932-43) ed C A Marris.

The postwar period saw the rise of a new generation of poets–Wellington poets James K Baxter, Alistair Campbell, W H Oliver and others centred on Louis Johnson, founder of *The New Zealand Poetry Yearbook* (1951-64). This group, more interested in urban than nationalistic issues, was seen as being in opposition to its predecessors, Brasch, Curnow and Glover but was perhaps less threatening than the latter group believed it to be. It was absorbed into Curnow's 1960 *The Penguin Book of New Zealand Verse* so that the two groups dominated New Zealand poetry until the introduction of postmodernism in the late sixties and early seventies. This last development came about through a number of avenues inclusive of courses in American poetry conducted by Wynstan Curnow and Roger Horrocks at Auckland University. From 1969 their students, Ian Wedde, Murray Edmond, Jan Kemp and their associates, burst spectacularly onto the scene and threatened to do to their predecessors the same as Curnow had done to his predecessors in 1945. *The Young New Zealand Poets* (1973), an anthology edited by Arthur Baysting brought wider recognition to the group which then put out a series of publications establishing its position. The situation had become extremely complex however and it was possible for poets of many persuasions to exist. Lauris Edmond, essentially a conservative with Georgian leanings, managed to find favour even while Alistair Paterson was arranging the highly successful 1976 visit of American poet Robert Creeley to demonstrate as he put it, 'the reality of postmodern and "open form" writing in New Zealand'.

During the same period and particularly from 1970, women writers assumed a greater prominence – a prominence made manifest by Riemke Ensing's 1977 anthology of women's writing, *Private Gardens*. Similarly there was a surge in poetry by Maori and Pacific Islanders as exemplified by Witi Ihimaera's anthologies of Maori writing,*Te Ao Marama* vols 1, 2, and 3 published between 1980 and 1993, and the two anthologies of Pacific writing, *Lali* (1980) and *Nuanua* (1995), edited by Albert Wendt.

In the eighties C K Stead, turned towards postmodernism, publishing the influential essay From Wystan to Carlos. Again, there was contention between the younger Auckland University group of poets and their elders, with some members of the former denigrating Stead's essay and Paterson's *Fifteen Contemporary New Zealand Poets* (1980) as either mistaken or unnecessary. The rest of the decade was taken up by a consolidation of postmodern influences and in the early nineties, the development of a semiotic influence in New Zealand writing. Leading the latter development Alan Loney who put out the postmodern magazine *Parallax* in the late seventies and early eighties, went through a period of relative silence until his periodical *A Brief Description of the Whole World* made an appearance in the 1990's. The most recent development has been the rise of GenerationX, led by Mark Pirie who in 1998 edited and published the iconoclastic anthology *New Zealand Writing: the Next Wave*, and has since then founded the publishing house, Headworx which has published such outstanding recent arrivals as Jack Ross, Simon Williamson who committed suicide at the age of thirty, and many others.

The proliferation of literary journals over the last ten years has resulted in an outpouring of poetry in a wide variety of forms. In Wellington this development has been led by Bill Manhire of Victoria University and by *Sport*, a literary journal published by Victoria University Press. *Landfall*, established by Charles Brasch in 1945 continues to operate as a bi-annual coming out of Otago University, while Louis Johnson's *New Zealand Poetry Yearbook* has evolved into this country's leading poetry magazine and an international journal of note. These developments in conjunction with the internet have resulted in New Zealand writing becoming an important part of the international poetry scene and a developing influence on poetry.

Alistair Paterson

From the 1875- shippings Arrival File

Mrs Honey, Miss de Quincy, Ah Foo
4 in steerage and 25 armed constabulary
after four days largely clement travel
made the embryonic port and berthed.

A fledgling reporter of a fledgling paper
pencilled their names as they stepped ashore
perhaps noting the curious aspect of Ah Foo
or asking him to confirm the spelling.

Masters Lightfoot and Morton, later seen
at the assembly, lightly tripping with
the Misses Christiansed (something
uncertain, shimmering about the name

like a scintilla of doubt) Mr Nuttman
Mrs Wyergang: the names they brought
in each new coastal arrival seemed
promising more than the place could deliver

but would in time fulfil. Mrs Breach
with hint of war, Miss Bath and the
ubiquitous Messrs Rain and Snow
not to mention the likely outcome: Miss Demnent

who nonetheless showed no trepidation
bringing her rich carpetbag ashore
and that essential colouring: 2 American darkies
like the denizens of a music hall or

decades of industry: 25 plate-layers for
Brodgen and Son. Still, as the waves
receded, let the present concentrate on
the most needed: Mr Fox, Mr Barleyman, Mr Gout

and Mrs Eagle: all qualities solutions would
be required for. And perchance supplied by
Miss Mountchal, Messrs Tutty and Worn
Mr Shalders, Mr Tasson, whatever they might stand for.

Elizabeth Smither

Kool Notes For You

i buy George Barker
on flinders street
and study the pink/blue cover
in the half-dark. but

thinking of you,
not the cover, &
then mixing them up,
regardless...

George is standing
or leaning
into the light, a fag
in hand,

not really smiling
or trying to be any-
thing but being 'him-
self'.

i'm reminded of you,
that natural cool.
i'd like to be like that.
like 'you'

'the you holding the letter,'
that's what you said,
George knows it,
i know it, & you

said it. melbourne is
terrific, lots of gardens & parks,
beautiful at night, & especially
i like the river.

Mark Pirie

RIVERTON BEACH POEM FOR TIM

Riverton Beach? I was there once
for a family reunion,
stood on algae-skinned rock

facing the sea, and thought
I was a child playing
by the cool water, sun-tanned

glassy-eyed, out with the family,
though it wasn't me
that was playing there,

just my father - part of
my history, but, later,
I stood there too, and nowhere

did we skim stones …
My father was older now,
with son-in-tow. Me, learning

the far fragments of past,
feeling his years grow colder,
memory passing like a falling star.

Mark Pirie

Two National Myths

for M.H. Holcroft

1. *Mapping the Land*

The macrocarpas, kowhai
and tree-ferns glisten
thru the window of
Curnow, Brasch & Co.

They lie fingering the rain
that sweeps over hooded hills;
mist comes early in the fault-
ed valleys and hovers above

the sea. Here the trampers
find the broad boughs of plants
and trees, the wonder of
the forests, the glaciers,

peaks and mountains, and
the poetry of rivers, lakes,
that otherworldly sublime,
the hard-pressed landfall.

2. *Eyeing the Broader Perspective*

From a house in Welling-
ton, a young man spies a
girl in black-and-white
puts down his poetry

book and follows her
down the street, he
thinks of *love*, the physical stuff, how her skirt

ripples in the breeze,
how her legs flash apart,
reminding him of Paris
in the spring-time, of

Baudelaire, of how his
death drum beckons
beyond this land, beyond
his town's narrow seas...

Mark Pirie

No Ordinary Son
Hone Tuwhare goes north

An august occasion at Auckland University. Academics, literati and some of the country's most illustrious poets have gathered to pay tribute to Allen Curnow, who died last year, and to witness the awarding of a posthumous honorary doctorate. Poets such as Bill Manhire and C K Stead have already read Curnow poems; now Hone Tuwhare - who, with Curnow's death, has become the most senior New Zealand poet - takes the stage. He looks a bit stooped and frail. There has already been a ripple of concern when he left the room hastily, helped out by Manhire, and though he's back now, he needs a bit of help getting up to the rostrum.
Once there, he seems to spend an eternity fossicking with spectacles and papers. The audience waits patiently, tolerantly, of-course-he's-an-old-man-nowishly. But then Tuwhare leaves off fossicking and stumbles away from the rostrum as if disoriented. A murmur of anxious sympathy hovers on lips all round the room. Has the old fellow lost it altogether? Not a chance. Suddenly he swivels, strikes a karate-like pose and roars at the audience: 'Tihei mauriora!' - then thunders a traditional Maori salutation before returning to the rostrum and reading his contribution with perfect vigour.

So there. You can never be quite sure where you are with Hone Tuwhare. Crouching tiger, hidden taniwha, he's an off-the-wall kaumatua, the wise old man with a gleam in his eye and a slingshot in his pocket. Or, as fellow poet Glenn Colquhoun puts it, 'He's a guerrilla poet. He sets you up and then takes the piss out of you.' And he keeps learning new tricks: though he's rather deaf these days, you can't escape the sneaking suspicion that the deafness is a moveable feast - a useful excuse when peace and quiet are preferred. He says it himself: 'When I don't want to hear someone, I say you're speaking in the wrong ear.'
Deafness and a touch of the flu aside, the man's in pretty good shape. In fact, if you were picking a first XV of New Zealand writers - a sort of literary All Blacks - there's no question about it: Tuwhare would just have to be the halfback. The Byron Kelleher of New Zealand poetry, he has the right nuggety build and feisty attitude, and he's pretty nippy round the scrum of life, good at spotting poetic ball and swinging it wide. By now he'd also probably have kicked this metaphor in the shins. A crowd

favourite, he's no stranger to the sin bin either. For nearly 40 years, cajoling, chortling, fulminating, his lusty poetic voice has made most other New Zealand poets seem dry and desiccated by comparison. He seduces women in verse, uses bodily functions like parts of speech, talks to the elements as though they were his mates or his rivals in love. (i) *Hey, you, Tangaroa, ocean. YOU, with the blubbery, soft-thwacking gums working...* (i) A boilermaker for much of his working life, he has been regularly published since 1964 (and believes he still has a couple of books left in him, too), while relishing his role as a public performer. As Ken Arvidson once said, 'I don't think Tuwhare has ever published anything that he couldn't bring to life on a public platform.'

For the past few years, however, he has been living in relative seclusion in his crib at Kaka Point on the Otago coast, happy to be a southern man. Which made it quite a challenge for Colquhoun to get him to come north and do a poetry reading tour through Northland, where Colquhoun himself lives and works as a doctor. For nearly two years Colquhoun wrote letters and sent messages to no avail; finally he turned to the *Listener* for help: six months ago we accepted and published his poem 'An invitation to Hone Tuwhare to attend a poetry reading in Northland', which began:

>Kaka Point! Give us back our boy!

and continued:

>Send back his stubby limbs!
>send back his round belly!
>send back his bursting tinana fat with kutai,
>kina, fish-heads, salt and words.
>Ngapuhi! Go and get our boy.

Well, it worked. No one had to go and get him; eventually, thanks not least to the help of Glennis Woods, who runs the Kaka Point shop, Tuwhare, at 79, came north under his own steam.

Back to Northland, where he was born (in Kaikohe in October 1922) and spent the first few years of his life; back to Ngapuhi country and the home of his hapu, Ngati Korokoro, in the Hokianga; back, you might say, to his roots. He is, as Colquhoun's poem says, no ordinary son. So with all that in mind, the tour was billed as 'A Sentimental Journey'. You get the picture: great man returns to the scenes of his childhood...cue violins...get out your handkerchiefs...

'Bullshit,' says Tuwhare. 'It's a learning thing for me. I don't know this area, I've only once before gone through, but it didn't mean substantially much to me.'

The fact is that Tuwhare has spent most of his life avoiding Northland. Like fellow Northlander Ralph Hotere, the artist, he lives about as far in New Zealand as it's possible to get from Northland - in rural Otago. One big reason for that is that, as he gets older, he fears being trammelled by tribal ties and oversolicitous relatives. He has never forgotten how, when he was five, and his mother had died, and her body lay in the house, people stood around drinking and, in his words, skiting that 'I looked after her better than you did' and 'I'm closer to her than you are'.

Maybe he just feels lucky to have survived the north in the first place, and still doesn't want to tempt fate. As Janet Hunt says in her excellent biography of Tuwhare, he was the only one of the five children his parents had together to survive infancy (one swallowed rat poison, another fell into a cesspit and drowned). He thinks there must have been a curse on the family, because of relatives' disapproval of his father's choice of a wife. 'I was the only one that survived,' he says, 'because my uncle gave me his name.'

He's also uneasy about being exposed to too much mihi, or Maori speechmaking, and specifically asked Colquhoun to get someone else to reply to welcome speeches, even though strictly speaking it's his place to do them when he's the chief guest of honour. 'I'm not trained up on replies and that, in a Maori sense,' he claims, adding that he's not even a fluent speaker of te reo and that 'if I want to write anything in Maori, I have to rely on good old Williams (the dictionary)'.

Plus, Colquhoun's very public call to him in the *Listener* left him with mixed feelings.

'I was a bit embarrassed about that, goodness gracious. He goes overboard, dammit. God and bloody hell. Still, I thought I'll come up here and he might be an interesting bugger to meet. If he's a doctor I can get free pills off him. Well, indeed he has.'

Sitting in a car high above Omapere, looking out over the spectacular Hokianga heads, I ask Tuwhare if it's a special feeling for him, being back in the north. 'No, no, not really,' he replies, and starts talking warmly instead about his beloved Otago, the snow-capped mountains, the beauty of the South Island. Kaka Point has surely got him for good now.

Still, he has come. And despite the gruff refusal to wallow in sentimentality, he clearly has deep feelings about being back. He would have to have a heart of flint, too, not to be moved by the affection shown him on all sides. 'My hero!' one woman even cries on meeting him; many gaze on him with something like awe. With his impish ways and non-PC jokes (spotting a phallic microphone boom, he exclaims to a room full of polytech students: 'Jeez, that's a long one, I wish I had one that size'), he's like some lewd Greek statue come to life, half god, half man, half Zeus, half Pan.

And, like a god making sport with mortals, he has come with his very own juggler. Visiting his son on Waiheke Island on the way north, Tuwhare met juggler Tim Newman and, after seeing him perform, spontaneously invited him on the tour. Which already includes the divinely-voiced singer Mahina Kaui, who, together with partner Lavinia Kingi and guitarist Nopera Pikari, forms the heart of the Big Belly Woman Arts Trust; and Colquhoun himself - likeliest contender among younger New Zealand poets for Tuwhare's mantle of people's poet. Before long, they're augmented by the redoubtable Aunty Maud Gubb, a living legend on the banjo-ukulele. Put all these talented people together, plug them into the Tuwhare dynamo, and from day one the whole entourage is generating good times, warmth and aroha like a hot-wired hui on wheels (see 'A week in the life').

Tuwhare himself, though, is forever backing into the limelight. His natural modesty and humility, drummed into him by his father when he was young, constantly wars with an urge to make serious mayhem with people's expectations. At readings, he plays the reluctant bride who virtually has to be dragged to the altar. When the time comes for him to step up to the microphone, it's always 'Who, me?' or 'Again??' accompanied by a slightly desperate look around as if someone else far more qualified should be volunteering instead. Once at the mike, however, he puts on a totally professional show, delivering his poems with force and fire.

Part of this attitude stems from a belief that being a poet is nothing special - that anyone could do it if they put their mind to it, and that therefore he should not be treated any differently. He's quoted in Hunt's book as saying: 'I do not consider the social function of a creative writer as superior to that of a tradesman boilermaker, a boilermaker's assistant, or better than that of a menial worker who switches on the tea urn and washes out the lavatories.' No one, he says, should regard it as a remarkable that he, a former boilermaker, should have become a successful poet: 'I mean to say, what the fuck's wrong with that! Bloody hell, it's not a monopoly of academics!'

He tries to convince the Rawene Polytech students that they too can write poems, provided the following prerequisite is met: 'You've got to love books in the first place to be able to handle words. These are the tools of expressions, words, the basic tools, like a pick and shovel, right?'

Asked when he first started falling in love with poetry and wanting to write it, he replies: 'When I fell in love with the subject, who was a female, you see. It has to be from real things you know around you. It doesn't just float out of the air. Rangi doesn't help you that way, no. It has to be people around you, preferably of the opposite sex – man, woman, old people, people who brought you up, wise people, people who did something bad to you. Remember them, honour them with your writing.'

Lovers, friends, relations, gods, devils, the forces of nature about us - all are honoured and upbraided in Tuwhare's own writing. The poems are, by any standard, extraordinary. Over the years they've become ever more dithyrambic and discursive. (i) *But where IS the Sun? Where IS he hiding? Jesus Christ-Mary-and-Joseph, when I find him I will surely trash him*. (i) The titles alone suggest a relationship with the environment that few of us would aspire to, let alone conceive of: 'The sun is a truant', 'A hongi for you too, Spring', 'I hold rhetorical hands with the sea'.

'He's maverick,' says Colquhoun. 'He's come out of left field. He's Maori but he's written poems in high English - English that we don't use any more - and I guess that comes from the fact that the Bible was his primary text, particularly in his early poems. But what I love is his juxtaposition of beautiful English with the hardcase colloquial New Zealand vernacular.'

Above all, Tuwhare's poetic imagination centres on the sea: his mind goes in and out with the tide, his poems are seafood for the soul. When I ask him one of those naff questions journalists sometimes ask, viz, do you have a philosophy of life, he omits to mention the usual ethical systems and replies: 'I just think in terms of sea and the food and the bounty that Tangaroa is able to give me and indeed humanity. Every race in the world is dependent on the sea too as well for fish and shellfish. It's a great saviour, it's a hell of a saviour.' These musings then segue into a rhapsody about South Island potatoes and the bounty of the land.

By God, he loves his seafood. During the tour, at a memorable dinner hosted by Heather Randerson at her Omapere home, Tuwhare and old friend Pat Hohepa eat virtually nothing but fish. The rest of us help ourselves to meat, pasta, vegetables and salad, but the two older men down the end of the table crunch their way through mouthfuls of mussels, sea-eggs, fish-heads. By the end of the meal there's nothing on Tuwhare's plate but a small mountain of bones.

He loves Kaka Point too. The local people, he says, are good to him: 'They're kind because I wasn't cheeky, I wasn't a typical Ngapuhi showoff, you know, and I was humble... In fact at Otakou marae on Otago peninsula those people got to like me and in the end they got me to speak on their side to any visitors.'

This winter, having been dependent on a gas-bottle heater up to now, he's getting a fireplace put in at the crib, and is looking forward to being warmed by real flames instead of 'burbling gas'. Meantime, 'the electric blanket gets a thrashing, by Christ, it's on nearly all the time'.

Tuwhare is typically dry-eyed about the prospect of his own death. The last thing he wants is an elaborate funeral with mass mourning and public fuss. 'I don't want to tangi and all that crap,' he says. 'Well, not crap, some people like it that way; but not me. I like to have a say how I go without bothering anybody. It's a private sort of thing. I'll just make arrangements with my lawyer and undertaker.'

He just wants to slip away quietly at a time of his own choosing (he supports euthanasia), and have his ashes scattered in five places - off Kaka Point, and in Otago, Wellington, Auckland and Hokianga harbours. As for what happens after that, his grandchildren are there to carry his spirit on. There's a grandson on Waiheke, for instance, who can barely walk at the moment, 'and on his tiny feet I'll still walk when I'm dead - okay? I'll walk into the future on his tiny little legs.'

Chuckling mightily, too, no doubt. And crunching happily on a fishhead.

Denis Welch

First published in the New Zealand Listener in April 2002

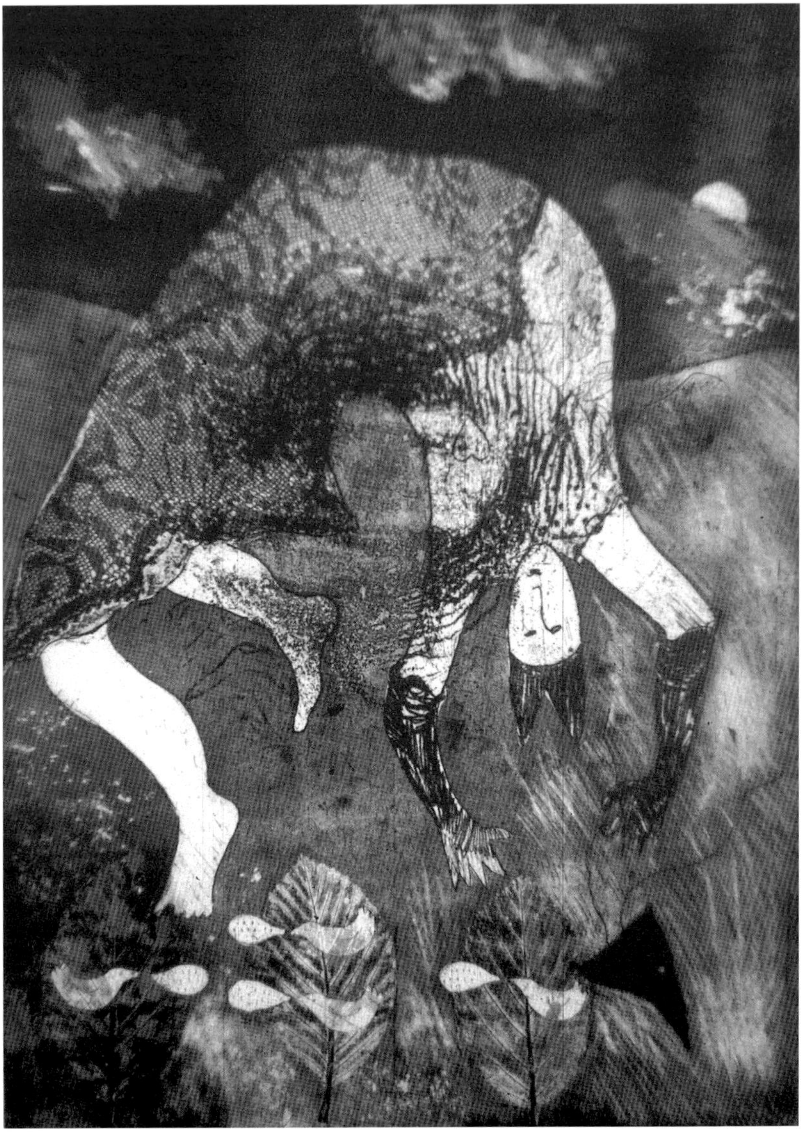

CANTERBURY GOLD

Fields of gold
sunshine ripe
crushed by expert hands
declared
ready for harvest.

'Can I sit with you, Grandad,
up high on the header?'

The fan turns
slicing head and stalk
row on flat row
churning, threshing
seeds to shutters
brown sacks
hooked, gaping, waiting.

'Quick, Grandad, quick;
three bags full,
close the shutters.'

Leather-tanned fingers,
deft, thread the needle,
fold and sew, fold and sew,
sacking 'pig ears'
to lift and throw.

Begin again,
hook and shutter,
watch the grain flow,
Dante's gold.

Smoko.
Dust air settles,
a tractor's shade,
black tea,
ginger crunch-
honey yellow,
yellow as the sun,
the sun hot,
the sky forever.

'Watch your little toes now,
pick your path, pick your path.'
Stubble sharp,
stripped straw lines
ejected, strewn.
Bulging bags
laden rich,
stand as stooks
from times past.

No scythe -
just Dad, Grandad,
me and the machine
begin again 'til day's end.
'Run rabbit, run rabbit.'
Just Dad, Grandad,
me and the land.

Canterbury gold.

Kay McGregor

The Empty Dovecote

beverage selection list propped against a pepper pot
sauvignon blanc just the right temperature
outside the conservatory the gardener's tight trousers
slumping in his chair, the bored child
rocking on the gazebo's pipe arch, a rose tendril
holidays - reading library books at the table - schoolboys
light on the meniscus - her half-empty glass
looking for somewhere to put the plant, the young girl
through the palings a rust-red roof
pot plants in a row on the garden seat
husband & wife's jaws chew in unison
different greens: kiwifruit, avocado, cucumber and pepper
crunched between the boy's toes a seed pod
a white butterfly flies towards the dovecote

Catherine Mair
Patricia Prime

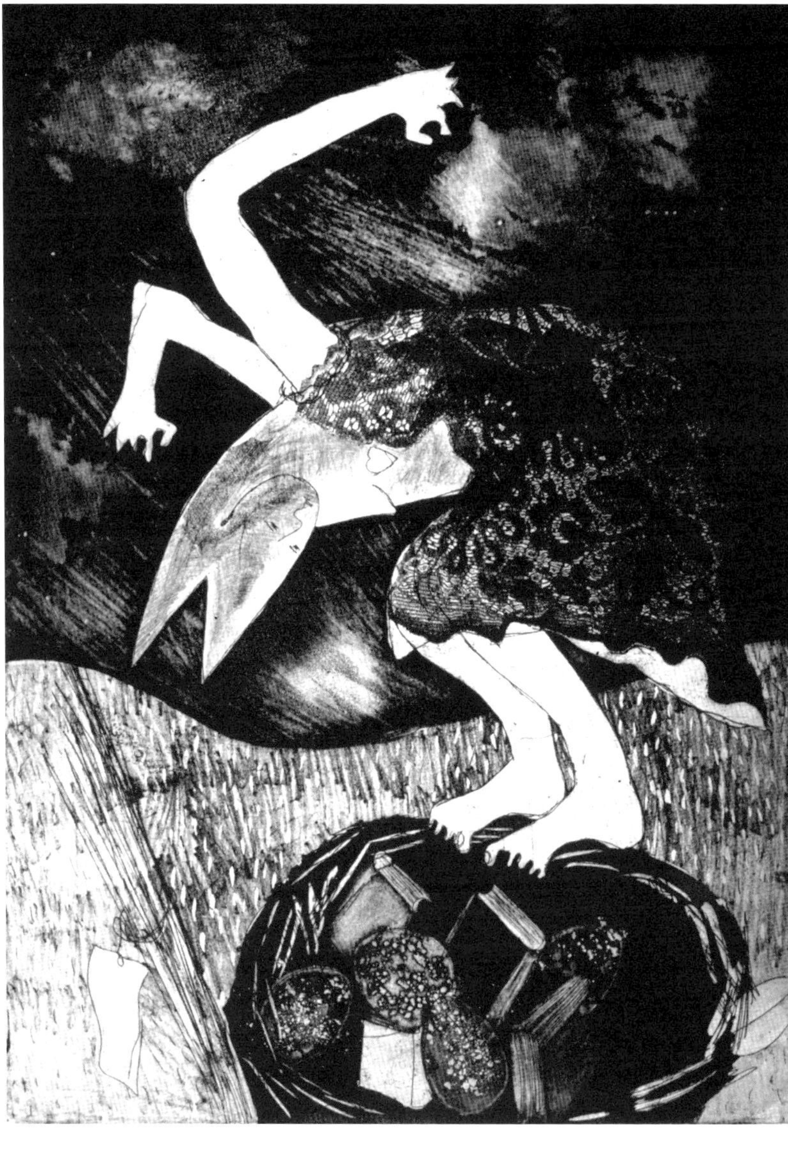

The Tent Factory

At ten o'clock the phone rings. The foreman brings the cordless over. Take ya time, he says. He's grinning. He's touched me twice, this morning, showing me how to work the eyeletting machine. Nothing obvious, maybe nothing at all, an accident. We'll see. I look after myself.

Melanie? How are you? How's your first day going? - I can hardly hear Daniel; a guy on a bench near me is cutting canvas with a blunt knife, the fibres parting reluctantly, loudly. Good, I say. Good. I look away from the phone and down the dim length of the factory, glad that Daniel can't see me here, see the grinning white ape of a foreman who's hanging around, just hanging around. Daniel. Why do I have to report to him? Do I ask him what he gets up to in that office of his? He wants to know everything. Am I enjoying the work? What exactly am I doing? Is it safe?

I squeeze my eyes shut. I'm gripping the phone too hard. His voice is tinny and insistent in my ear. I open my eyes, look at my watch. We're paid for what we do, not by the hour; this call is costing me money. But he's talking, talking, and I'm saying, yes, no, yes, no. He doesn't listen, doesn't get the message. Got to go now, I say. I've got to go. When I hang up, he's still talking.

You put the washer on the lower metal die. The eyelet slips on to the upper die. You put the canvas in the space between. Somebody has already marked on the canvas where the eyelet is to go. You stamp the pedal with your foot, and the upper die crashes down, the eyelet cuts through the canvas, pierces the washer and hits the lower die; the sharp edge curls back neatly on itself, securing the washer in place.

This is my job, at least for now. Later, if I prove myself, I'll go on to cutting, and maybe sewing. The canvas is heavy, dark green; it gets cut and folded and sewn into tents for the army. The green rubs off easily on to clothes and skin. Everyone is green.

There are No Smoking signs everywhere. Everyone smokes. We work, nine or ten of us, in a long, stuffy room, with yellow fluorescent tubes high above. The canvas is unrolled on a huge wooden bench that runs the full length down one side of the room. From the ceiling are suspended big wooden templates for making roofs, walls, wings. One of these is lowered by pulleys on to the canvas and a guy scampers over it, marking the canvas and cutting it to shape, then cutting where the windows are to go. The template is hoisted back up and the guy runs around the bench, folding and creasing the canvas with a wood block. Then he chucks the wall or whatever across the central aisle to the bench on the other side, where the machinists are.

The machinists are all women. They sit in holes in their bench, behind their machines. Each machine has been fitted with a safety guard, which each machinist has removed. The guards are around the needles; they get in the way, slow the women down. The canvas races under the first machine, then is hurled on to the next, and the next. And then the completed piece is thrown to me, and I stamp the eyelets in.

Daniel knows all this, now. All this I have told him. Tonight he will discuss it further. He will be stern about the smoking and the stripped safety guards. He will talk about toxicity of dyes. He will ask more about work processes, and suggest improvements.

He worries about me, Daniel does, and he's very protective. Every night he says to me, when we go to bed, I love you, Melanie. Every night, before we go to sleep, as if I might die before morning. I love you, Melanie. He doesn't expect an answer. So many stones in my pockets, he weights my pockets with stones and leads me to the river.

The guy who stamped eyelets before me, he never did anything else. He stamped eyelets for three years. Never missed a beat, the foreman says. Then one day he didn't turn up. He didn't turn up all week. They heard nothing, they thought he'd topped himself. He was moody, the foreman says, kept himself to himself. No sense of humour. Not like you. That's the third time he's touched me.

And ya know what? The foreman laughs. He hadn't topped himself. He got another job, got a job with a camping equipment outfit in Auckland. Making tents. He's still stamping eyelets!

This isn't very funny. I'm stamping eyelets, too, I haven't done it for three years, sure, but I've stamped eyelets for most of a day and I think about him, that guy with no sense of humour.

If you place the washer incorrectly, a little to one side instead of squarely on the die, the eyelet hits it wrong and everything mangles, the eyelet, the canvas and the washer together. You don't get a tidy, smooth hole; you've got to wrench the washer off with pliers, pull the eyelet out, and try again. You get bored stamping eyelets all day, so sometimes you put the washer to one side and crash the eyelet in, just so you get to use the pliers. The foreman knows this, and he's watching me. He's watching me all the time.

Daniel wanted, he wants kids. You should think about starting a family, his mother says. My mother says it, too. As if they have a right to say it, as if they were happy with what their husbands, their mothers bullied them into. Daniel smiles sheepishly at them, he puts his arm around my shoulder and smiles. More coffee? he asks. He is an attentive host. More coffee?

I'm plucking at the washer with the pliers but it's stuck fast. Then there it is, the foreman's hand closing briefly over mine, taking the pliers from me. The bent washer spins to the floor. The back of his hand is red, and covered with fine, black hairs. The pores are dark green.

There ya go, he says. Easy mistake. The other guy used to do it all the time. He grins his wide, wet grin at me again. He's too close, he's chewing mints, but his breath is not good.

Lemme show ya, he says. And he moves behind me and reaches around, puts the eyelet on the upper die. It's real easy, he says, and I can feel him now, against my back, as his other arm comes around, the washer in his hand. The phone is ringing.

Take it slow, he says, his voice a whisper, hot and wet in my ear. The phone is ringing, the machines are chattering like mad, comes the thump and rasp and slap of canvas from the cutting bench, everyone's going like the clappers. I can feel the heavy thud of his heart in my own chest. He thinks I'm his, for the taking, but he's wrong. I am not here, I am outside this, watching. The moment is coming, and I'm ready.

I stamp down hard. He pulls away real quick but is stopped, jerked back to me. Something is holding him here. And this young guy who's walking over with the phone falters, stops; he looks at the two of us like an idiot, his eyes bugging out of his head. He starts to shake, he comes no closer but holds the phone out to me desperately, like he just wants to deliver it over and get the hell away.

Melanie? Melanie? What - And it's funny, though the foreman's screaming now, really loud, I can hear Daniel, this small voice coming from the phone. What is it, Melanie? What's that noise?

Shut up, I say. Just shut up. But they don't, the machines have stopped but they are all shouting now, and the foreman screaming louder than any of them. No-one listens. I look down at the bright blood. Shut up, I say, and I put my fists against my ears, and I back away, I walk away from there.

Tim Upperton

HOW TO TALK TO A PEACOCK

he will not want to know
about the harsh whistle of oxygen
the gasp beneath the plastic face mask

he cannot anticipate things beyond
the immediate strut flounce and flourish
so if you don't mind
keep it light
      shining
keep it iridescent
don't mention the blood

the wail of distant ambulances
is an unnecessary distraction
he would prefer the deep silence
of black waters studded with lilies
their mute admiration

but if you must mention stethoscopes
(or calipers or scalpels)
just speak of them as
bright shiny objects
of things perhaps
with their own beauty
although not the beauty
of the fabulous eye

in his fan tail
(at which you must gasp)
of perfect feathers

James Norcliffe

TCHAIKOVSKY ENTERS A NEW AND DARKER PERIOD OF HIS LIFE

In his dream there is
a long avenue of yew trees.
They spike the late summer
evening like a succession
of sharp black grace notes.

An orange sun setting behind him
stretches his jagged shadow
on the rack of the pathway
and causes the pink pastilles
to glow with waxy promises.

Such pretty poison can
scarcely be borne. Crow fruit,
raven fruit: not to be thought
about were it not for the
shadow and shudder of wings.

At the end of the pathway
Darkness sighs and carefully
buttons his black greatcoat,
stubs out his last corona
and reaches for his hat.

'I'm going now,' he whispers.
'Close the door behind me.'

James Norcliffe

ANTIGONE IN THE HOT POOL

there she lies
puddled and slurped
in the embrace of warm water:
it's comforting

          amniotic

she is thinking of how
a photographer paddles a print
in the urine-scented hypo
fixing the image forever

so that the black flies basking
on a white wall will shine
for all time in the dim light,
and she thinks of the flies

how their iridescent blue
whine had gathered round her
as she carried that dead weight
up the groaning mountainside

her father's her brother's
so many cold mountains
now through the rising steam
she can see their white peaks

her escape lies that way
but this water is warm
as forgiving as a loofah
and soft as a sponge

she has made it fragrant
with her mother's perfume

James Norcliffe

Nuclear Free

It's over. I sip my tea and gaze at a cloudy sky. The clamour of voices, the feverish activity, is a silent afterimage. More than silence there is quiet. No checklists running through my head; no what-ifs, no sense of possible disaster. I am alone.

As a child I liked to lie on my back and turn slowly under a still sky, watching clouds form and break up like a cumulus Rorscharch. I could read the patterns, see animals, mountains, familiar faces, new forms of life. As to meaning I saw none, the shapes came and went, with no past and no future. At night I could see into the fathomless black strewn with stars.

I knew that the appearance of Pleiades' misty lights marked the New Year. Later, I learnt that behind the serenity of the night sky lay death and devastation. The hearts of these peaceful points of light harboured cataclysms of destruction. Some stars were a tumult of gas and fire; others were already dead. Many bright embers of the night were dimming memories, dreams that had not yet faded. And what from afar was beautiful, and could be celebrated with dancing was a very different kettle of fish in your own back yard.

Of course I didn't share these observations with the Glenview Committee for a Nuclear Free Waitemata. Everything was wrapped in the catchcries of the day. American imperialism. Nuclear free. National sovereignty. Our job was not to gaze into the heavens and wonder. We were struggling for the hearts and minds of the people.

The committee deliberated for weeks, debating ways of making our mark. Gary Clark wanted to occupy the council offices. Brian Stephens suggested a letter writing campaign. He read to us from a CK Stead story, about a man who used pseudonyms to conduct arguments with himself in the press. Gracie thought a public education day at the marae would get people along.

'It's a Treaty issue' she said. 'Aotearoa was nuclear free in 1840'.
We argued and debated. Then one night, as if illuminated by a beam from Alpha Centuari, we came upon a plan that was so elegant, so devastatingly simple, that we broke into insane laughter. An hour of feverish planning and the campaign to save the Waitemata was underway

A stroke of genius really. A nuclear free hangi. There'd been an American ship in that year, the *Southern Glory*. Three people arrested, the usual accusations. Letters to *The Herald* three to one for the cause, the *Star* two to one. We were on to a winner.

We invited George Bolstad, sitting Labour MP. He would declare the the Waitemata a Nuclear Free Zone. Gracie offered to get the meat. The boys would put the hangi down in her back lawn.

'One of my boys is at the works. We get a discount. Sometimes we get a bloody good discount.' Gracie laughed, sucking air over bare gums, shoulders shaking.

Good job we had Gracie on the committee. You had to do things right. Gracie was Nga Puhi. If anyone knew the Treaty Nga Puhi did. The phone rang constantly.

'You the guys having the hangi? Nuclear free? Good on you. Who needs that nuclear shit?'

We ticked off names, wrote down others. There was a call from Kevin O'Reilly, spokesman for the Workers' and People's Party.

'I'll be there. Gotta keep them honest. It's about time we stood up.'

Kevin stood up all right. Last year it was against George Bolstad.

'Bugger's in the wrong party. Right in there with big business. What does he do for working people? Bloody nothing.'

Kevin polled 127 votes.

There was an article in the *Weekender*. A picture of the planning committee. What a crew we looked. But we got a lot more calls that weekend. It was going well. A week to go.

On Tuesday I called on Gracie.

'She's up north.'

The boy was about seventeen, lithe and smooth skinned, a haze of black over his upper lip.

It's about the meat…for the hangi…'

'She'll be back in a few days.'

There were more phone calls to make. Peter Vukic was the main speaker. Old CND campaigner. Seven days in Mount Eden for civil disobedience. The man was a legend. Yes, he'd remembered. Speeches at 3pm; hangi at 3.30.

George Bolstad asked for some background on Peter Vukic.

'What's that story about the CND? Something about time in the Mount? Want to make sure I get the facts straight.'

The hall manager, *the Weekender*, another round of the committee.

Thursday, another call to Gracie. The boys would bring the meat on Saturday.

'Saturday! But the planning committe.. we decided...'

'I have to go. My Aunty's here.' It was like that with Gracie.

On Friday I picked up the hall key.

'Look like a big do! I saw it in the paper.' Mrs Shaw told me about the lights, how to work the Zip. 'And there's plenty of kleensacks in the cupboard.'

That night I went to bed late. The meat. Would Peter Vukic make a good speech? The key. The meat. Call Gary in the morning. I lay with my eyes open. From my bed I could see the sprinkle of Pleiades' lights. At this time of the year they drift in a low arc across the north sky, fading from me as I sink into sleep. There's hundred of them, but that night I could only count seven.

....

Saturday morning the phone rings early. It's Gary.

'Fine day. Looks good. Everything ok?'

I drive round to Gracie's place. No-one there. Back home to phone the committee. As a contingency we decide on fish and chips. It'll cost though, and we were supposed to be raising money.

There's a knock at the door. Gracie's asking if there's any firewood. The boys are already dumping armfuls of ti tree into the back of the Valiant.

'Yeah, sure.' I help with the ti tree. I don't ask about the meat.

By 3pm there must be a hundred people there. Gary has the mike working, the seats are lined up on the stage.

George Bolstad gives the first speech. 'I remember a story about Peter Vukic during the CND days….' He tells the story about Peter's seven days in Mount Eden.

Peter Vukic is softly spoken and passionate. People listen, saving their applause till the end. I slip out to the kitchen.

3.35. I hear Gary announcing that the hangi will be served next door. There's no sign of Gracie and the boys. Faces peer through the door. There's paper plates, bread and butter, orange cordial and tea. The Zip whistles. Then the phone. It's Gracie. One of the boys has to go somewhere. Can I come and help lift the hangi? A mad sprint up the street to Gracie's place. The Valiant is backed up to the lawn, tailgate down. Wisps of steam seep from the hangi. Mat is ready to pull the sacks off. We toss them aside, inhaling the aroma, faces glistening. With the baskets gone there is a bed of stones, scorched and steaming.

We drive down the hill to the hall. I sneak a glance at my watch. 3.55. Mat smiles.

'Should be good. Nice fresh hangi. Nice and hot.'

The Valiant rumbles up the drive. We carry the baskets inside. Already people have spilled into the kitchen, standing around in groups, some eating the bread. They press towards the table as we place the baskets. Steaming packets of meat, kumara and pumpkin.

I'm supposed to be looking after Peter Vukic. He's not in the kitchen but George Bolstad is there shaking hands. Its my job to see that Peter gets a meal. I take a plate of meat and vegetables and a drink, pushing my way through the crowd. Kevin O'Reilly has Peter backed up to a wall, explaining the Trotskyist position on nuclear energy. A stream of words tumble out. Saliva droops to his chin, smeared away by the back of his hand. Peter's eyes sparkle, but when he talks about nuclear energy the sparkle fades like a dying star, and his eyes burn with a fiery intensity.

I shake Kevin's hand. 'Hello Kevin, good to see you.'

I steer Peter away, handing him his plate of food. The photographer from the *Weekender* appears and we pose for photographs.

People are milling around picking the last scraps of kumara from their plates and sipping tea. I'm hungry, and the thought of the hangi food draws me to the kitchen.

The crowd has moved away from the tables, leaving crumpled tinfoil and a few pumpkin rinds scattered about. I rake through the piles of tinfoil and find a warm packet. Someone's taken the meat, but the pumpkin and kumara are warm and sweet.

I make a cup of tea. There's no milk so I have it black.

George Bolstad claps me on the back.

'Good show, good turnout.'

He's picking his teeth and wiping his mouth. '*The Herald* rang this morning. I gave them a statement. Good exposure this.'

He moves off to seek out hands to shake, shoulders to drape his arms over.

The crowd thins out. Gary and Brian are clearing tables, stuffing plates and cups into kleensacks. The baskets have gone. Everyone says great idea, good on you. Brian offers to take Peter Vukic home, leaving Gary and me to see off the remaining guests. Kevin O'Reilly is sitting at a table, drinking tea, and lecturing to a dwindling group. He's the last to go. The sun is sinking, lending an orange glow to the windows. We count the takings. I drop the key off to Mrs Shaw. 'Did you leave the kleensacks outside? All locked up?'

At home I make a cup of tea and slump into an armchair. The sky has clouded over and the world is engulfed in grey. There are no stars, but beyond lie the galaxies, the clouds of fire and light. Out there Pleiades is sweeping across space, this time unseen. There is no reminder of the dread energy of exploding suns, just the fading light and a trace of the aroma of kumara.

Tim O'Brien

PROPERGANDA

DESIGN FOR PRINT AND WEB

10 ST MARGARETS TERRACE
YORK YO1 9UW
T: **(01904) 620848**
E: **MAIL@PROPERGANDA.ORG**
W: **WWW.PROPERGANDA.ORG**

URUPA MOTUOPAE: the sign points
from taonga on the shore
sandstone carved with arrows
soul's corridor

Through Waikareao
through mud
through silt
through scuttling crabs
through shell-mosaic floor
Motuopae. Motuopae,
crypt-cluttered shore

A silent pa watches high
on terraced banks.
Across the flats
Motuopae sprawls in
titree, toi toi,
reed and flax

Crucifixes poke from scrub,
slabs of granite leer
Tombstone isle,
Motuopae,
awash in widow's tears.

Michael Lee

Urupa - means sorrow, mourning in Maori
Motuopae - in Maori every syllable is pronounced separately (like my surname) - thus 'mow-too-ope-eye'; thus Waikareao is 'why-kah-ree-oh'
Taonga - means a homestead
Pa - formerly the Maori fortified settlement, always built on a hill, and lived in communally
Titree, Toi Toi - native plants

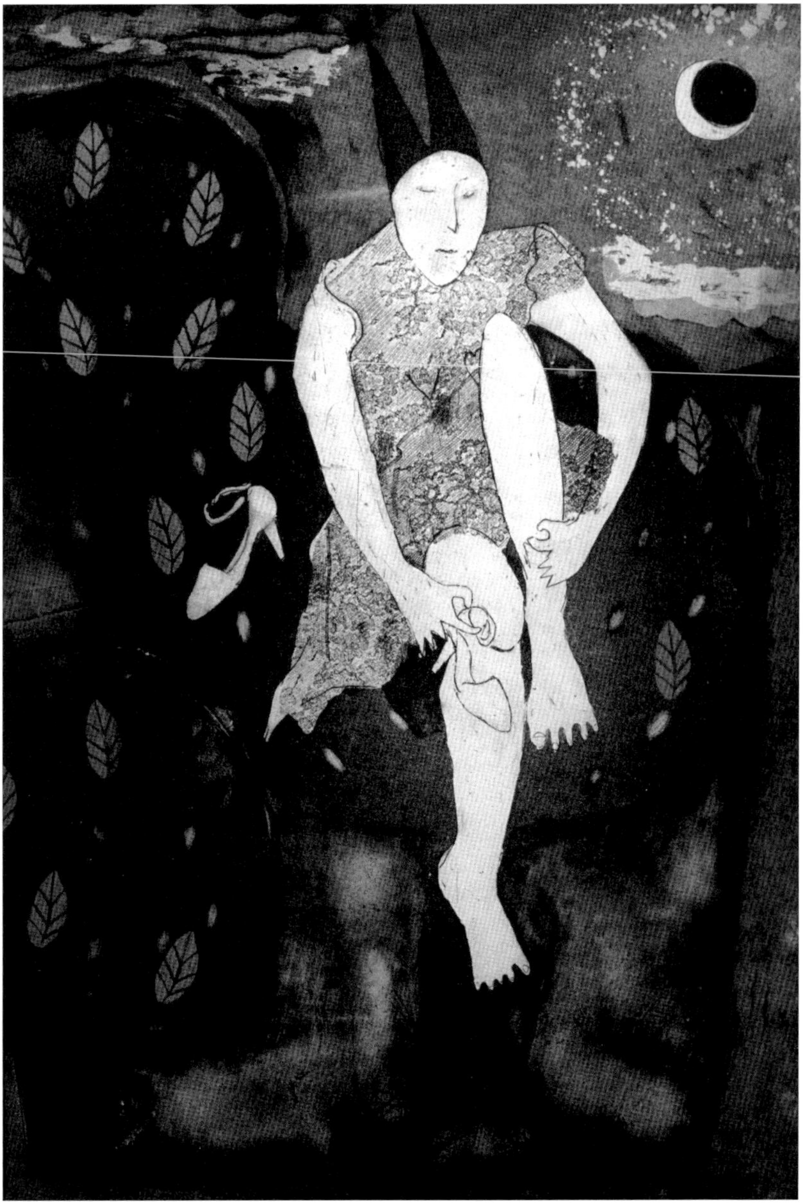

Cat and Mouse

Andrew watched me from the bed. I could feel his gaze on my back and I did my best to ignore it, to not turn round and shout '*What!*' I would not let him win. He said, in his soft, wheezy voice, 'I'm bored. Tell me a story.'

'I'm not your mother.'

'So? You're a storyteller.'

He almost got me with that but I could hear the slight edge in his voice so, even though his words crawled up my spine like little sharp knives, I ignored him.

'Aren't you?' he prodded, mildly. I imagined his eyes – a far too beautiful mixture of green and hazel - watching the shape of me with lazy interest.

I would not let him distract me. I had words to snare, to put down in order on the blank screen in front of me. I could have moved the computer out to the sun-porch or into the spare bedroom or even the living room but love anchored it firmly where it was, in the bay window of the master bedroom. I imagined how I looked to Andrew – a fuzzy shadow in front of a small pale square in front of a bigger, gleaming square. Light and dark moving in a haze of glimmers and gleams, like fish slithering through water. But no colour, the colours were first to go.

Andrew sighed, theatrically, and scrabbled at his duvet, also theatrically. I knew this without looking, from the sounds of the linen squeaking and the duvet rustling, and from knowing him so well it was like fitting inside my own skin.

'Once upon a time,' he said, 'there was a non-magical, very small, kingdom-that-wasn't in a land very close to you.'

I typed *magic* on my computer screen, but the word didn't conjure up anything special.

'And in this kingdom-that-wasn't, there lived a very selfish girl called Lou-,'

'And a very selfish man called Andrew.' *Damn.* Sometimes I felt like a trout being played by an expert. A rainbow, of course.

Andrew smirked at me behind my back. I could feel it. 'And what did Andrew and Lou do in their kingdom-that-wasn't?' he asked.

'Andrew had a nice little sleep so Lou could get some work done.'

'Work.' This word arrived on a snort. *Work.* 'That's the most important thing to you, then?'

'Do you *want* me to drug you senseless?'

'Charming.' Pause, and with perfect timing, 'yes please.'

37

I gave up. *Only for now*, I told myself, but knew the day's words were gone, meaning and shape had swirled away, leaving me heavy and lost. Words. They were all crap, anyway. What did they change?

There are drugs and drugs. Legal, illegal, helpful, harmful, but in the end, who cared as long as something made you feel better, for at least that moment? Not so long ago Andrew had rolled his own joints, but his hands had become thin, translucent little claws so now I did it for him.

His eyes were dark. They glistened with pain and I saw his need was real, so I held the joint to his mouth. His lips were dry and peeling. Painful. 'Thanks,' he said. Smoke trickled from his nostrils as he relaxed, his eyes closed.

His eyelids were big, bruised eggs. I watched him in the silence that gathered around us like shadows.

'What time is it?' he said.

'What time does it feel like?' I asked. I didn't understand this compulsion of his to always know the time. What did it matter? Summer, winter, morning, or night, what could it matter?

And yet, and yet

Who wouldn't want a life mapped by the pathway of time?

'Four o'clock,' I said. 'Morning.' He nodded, and I felt cruel. 'Afternoon, really.'

He laughed weakly, a snuffling of sound in his chest and throat. The joint was doing its work. I slid a glance at the clock. It was 2.30pm and Angie would be home soon from school.

'Liar,' he said. 'You'd be gone if it was.'

'Maybe. Or maybe I've had to stay late because Angie's been hit by a bus.' His bruised-egg eyelids twitched. 'Good. I'll get the insurance money.'

'Not that you'll live long enough to spend it.' No, that was going too far. 'Sorry.'

He squinted at me. 'Why? It's the truth'.

'Shut up Andrew.'

'Do you remember,' he said, 'the ghosts of Christmas past? Snow and hot mince pies and getting a sled…' His voice slurred into silence, and I remembered falling off that very sled, and purple-tipped fingers and crying with the cold as I floundered home. Mum wrapping me up in her arms and kissing me better.

I wanted my mother.

'Sure,' I said.

The joint had gone out, but sweet sickly smoke filled the room. Angie would go ballistic. Andrew went to sleep, slack-jawed and snoring softly. His lungs bubbling in time. I could have written then, if I'd wanted, but I sat and watched him while the pain in my chest stretched out long cold fingers and crushed me.

We'd made an agreement, Andrew and I, when we were fourteen and our best friend had been hit by a drunk driver and turned into a vegetable.

We'd sworn statements, made promises, signed a contract:

I, Andrew Stuart Melvor will not allow you, Louisa Jane Melvor, to exist as a vegetable.

I, Louisa Jane Melvor will not allow you, Andrew Stuart Melvor, to exist as a vegetable.

Don't be ridiculous, our mother had said.

And yet, and yet.

Doors banged on the far side of the house, and footsteps clumped up the hallway. Angie. She sounded like an old, old lady who had to force one foot in front of the other but she came into the room quietly enough, a slim neat-figured woman with a mass of thick shining hair and full, pouting lips. I couldn't reconcile her image with her job. How could she look like that and teach five-year old kids?

She gave a cool smile toward me, and I gave a cool nod in her direction.

'How's he been?' she said. She leaned over Andrew and stroked his face, smoothed his hair and kissed his poor clawed hand, held it to her cheek.

'It's been a good day,' I said. Meaning, for him.

He opened his eyes, squinted toward Angie. 'Hi babe,' she said, and a deep, shimmering joy spread across his face.

I turned away to pack up my things. My fingers felt fat as I scrabbled up pencils and pens, and shuffled papers together. Behind me, Angie said, 'I went Christmas shopping at lunch-time.'

Don't talk about the fucking future is what I thought. Andrew said, 'Cool. What this year?'

Last year it had been a beach theme – a paua shell and driftwood decorated table out on the deck, paper-maché fish hanging from the pergola. The year before, the theme was elegance, with polished silver and white linen, tiny gifts wrapped in gold paper. The year before that a country & western celebration with gingham covered tables, a turkey in the oven and pumpkin pie.

imagine, a Christmas tree
from the vege patch
with thin jagged leaves (not pine)
round, red globes (not glass)
sunlight (not stars)

This year, I wanted angels and heavenly choirs, a promise of things to come.

I wanted the ghosts of Christmas past, that old land where snow fell and fires roared a welcome and the future stretched away with beckoning, seductive fingers. What was the point of a Christmas when there was only a past left to consider.

Angie said, 'It's a surprise. You'll have to wait and see.'

I dropped my bag and stared at her. Was she mad? Christmas was six weeks away. Forty-two long, aching days, one thousand and eight hours. Sixty thousand minutes… three and a half million heartbeats.

Andrew rolled his head toward me. 'Lou? You're still here?' He half-lifted his free hand and I went and took it, folded it between my own two. Angie and I stood either side of the bed, looking at the man we both loved.

'My two favourite women,' he said. 'I'm glad you'll have each other.'

'Don't be so melodramatic,' I said.

'Of course we will,' said Angie, and managed to shoot daggers at me while she kept her voice soft and light.

Men could be so stupid. Angie was jealous of me. 'No need to be,' Andrew had said, but of course, there was. I was his twin. I filled a place in him no one else could, not even his lover. But then, I was jealous of Angie. She filled a place in Andrew that I could never reach.

'I'll see you tomorrow,' I said, and bent to kiss Andrew's grey, clammy cheek. 'Love you,' I said.

'Ditto, kid.'

Angie walked me out. The air between us simmered with bad-temper and angry words. I hissed, 'You have no right to promise him Christmas.'

She swivelled eyes like blue marbles toward me. 'He has to have something to look forward to.'

'You stupid shallow bitch. This is what he's got to look forward to; becoming fully blind and completely paralysed and choking on the fluid in his own lungs. Do you really think,' I was so angry I was spitting out words. 'your stupid freaking tinsel is going to make any difference?'

'Goodbye,' said Angie. 'Thank you for coming.'

I hated this woman. 'Don't you dare thank me. I come for Andrew, not you.'

'And I,' she said, 'put up with you for Andrew. Not me.'

There wasn't much subtlety between Angie and me.

There was honesty between Andrew and me. 'Be kind,' he said. His chest wheezed and bubbled as he choked out the words. 'It's hard for her.'

'And a piece of cake for me?'

He opened his poor bruised eyes and looked at me without seeing. 'No. But you've had me longer.'

Which was true, and a gift she could never share.

'Cold,' said Andrew.

I pulled up his blankets and tried not to let him hear me cry. Sunlight striped the room in bright golden bars, bathed his bed in warmth.

It rained a few days later, from great writhing clouds that swooped over the hills and poured through the streets like death itself. In spite of sunflowers bought from a florist's and Mozart on the CD, Andrew's bedroom was oppressive. It was a bad day, a day when each breath he took bubbled and wheezed and his hands lay by his side, trembling, when the oxygen machine hissed in the corner. The kind of day when I sat beside his bed, afraid to touch him because he hurt so much.

I, Louisa Jane Melvor will not allow you, Andrew Stuart Melvor, to exist as a vegetable. Or suffer agony.

When Angie came home, she took my place and leaned her cheek toward his, only a breath between them. 'Andrew,' she said, 'the storm's passed, can you tell? The sun's coming out. It'll be better tomorrow, you'll see. You'll see.'

'Must you make empty promises?' The words were out before I could stop them and she looked at me, her eyes dazed and hurting.

'I have to hope,' she said. 'Can't you see that Lou? *We* have to hope.'

She turned back to Andrew. 'Darling,' she said, 'I thought we'd go traditional this year, what do you think? Get a real tree with fake snow, and put a nativity scene on the mantel, hang socks by the fire. What do you think?'

I wanted to say, I think Christmas will be way too late. But I didn't. Andrew lay quietly, the rise and fall of his chest easing, the strain slipping out of his face. It was time for me to leave. 'Love you,' I said, and I swear his lips moved, *ditto, kid*.

Sue Emms

THE WORLD HEAD QUARTERS OF THE VERB:
THE WELLINGTON WRITERS' WALK

It's true you cannot live here by chance, you have to do and be, not simply watch or even describe. This is the city of action, the world headquarters of the verb.

These are the words that Lauris Edmond uses to explain her feelings for her city. She is one of eleven writers chosen to represent the richness of Wellington writing in the first phase of Wellington Writers Walk that was completed on the Wellington waterfront last year. The sense of activity that Edmonds saw in Wellington is a feature of the Walk.

Like many of the writers, Wellington is my adopted home. Unlike them, I struggle to find the words for what I feel about this city. For me the Walk turns out to be more than a stroll around a picturesque waterfront. It becomes another stage in an immigrant's journey.

Illustration Lauris Edmond 'The Active Voice'

A few surprises await as I make my way to the start of the walk at the Chaffers Marina. There are no brass ringed memorials recording births and deaths but, instead, a lively collaboration between literature, typography, architecture and the environment. Each text sculpture is a quote from the writer's work. Designer and typographer Catherine Griffiths won a prestigious national design award for her work on this project. Her response was to create a series of imposing concrete typographic sculptures that interact beautifully with the busy harbour and city that surround them and give them life. The sites have been carefully selected to complement that interaction. So sometimes that means that this is less of a walk but more a voyage of discovery, as much of Wellington and its harbour as of the writers. Better to let some of them speak, some in prose and some in poetry, although the difference is not always easy to distinguish in these sculptured versions of their words.

Katherine Mansfield, one of the few writers selected who was actually born in Wellington is at the start of the Walk. She looks across the harbour towards her birthplace in Thorndon. What would she make of the city now? The wind, at least, would be familiar to her:

> *Their heads bent, their legs just touching, they stride like one eager person through the town, down the asphalt zigzag where the fennel grows wild. The wind is so strong that they have to fight their way through it, rocking like two old drunkards.*

The Mansfield sculpture is flat but there is an invitation to read and flick your eyes up to encompass that harbour and Thorndon beyond.

James K. Baxter is a little more difficult to locate and he would be startled to find himself in the pool outside the Te Papa museum complex that dominates this part of the waterfront. In the end, it is just a matter of turning your back on the harbour to see his words:

> *I saw the Maori Jesus*
> *Walking on Wellington Harbour.*
> *He wore blue dungarees*
> *His beard and hair were long.*
> *His breath smelt of mussels and paroa.*
> *When he smiled he looked like the dawn.*

The letters are three-dimensional and sit just below the surface of the lake but still attract light and shadow. Ducks play scrabble with the letters. And, always, over your shoulder is the harbour.

Robin Hyde came to Wellington as a child and at seventeen became a reporter for *The Dominion*. Her autobiographical novel *The Godwits Fly* explores the theme of hunger for England where she eventually died, tragically, aged 33. Her sculpture, also on the perimeter of Te Papa, is more about the writer than where she is from.

Circa Theatre is one of two professional theatres in the city and it is not difficult to find playwright and theatre critic, Bruce Mason, here. The surprise, perhaps, is that his sculpture sits flat in the paving and lacks some of the flamboyance of his writing. There is no such problem with Bill Manhire, poet, short story writer and teacher of writing. His succinct message is suspended across wharf supports:

> *I live at the edge*
> *of the universe,*
> *like everybody else.*

As the sitting sun picks out the sharp edges of the letters, I remember that I am standing near an earthquake fault line and the waterfront itself sits on reclaimed land.

Bill Manhire Milky Way Bar
Photo credit, Bruce Connew, Network Photographers

Tucked away down by the boat club and down the road from her beloved Hongoeka Marae, is Patricia Grace. She is, with Witi Ihimaera, a leading figure in the emergence of Maori fiction in English although novels such as *Potiki* do have passages in Maori. The nomination of *Dogside Story* for the Booker Prize long list is an indication of a wider audience for her writing. She picks up the theme of the wind and Wellington at the edge:

> *I love this city, the hills, the harbour, the wind that blasts through it. I love the life and pulse and activity, and the warm decrepitude. There's always an edge here that one must walk which is sharp and precarious, requiring vigilance.*

Whatever your point of entry - by ferry from the South Island, by air or by road there is a sense of revelation when you arrive in this city for the first time. The weather will decide if you are to be gently, or violently, seduced. Here is Maurice Gee:

> *Then out of the tunnel and Wellington burst like a bomb. It opened like a flower, was lit up like a room, explained itself exactly, became the Capital.*

To read Gee's words one faces back towards the city and my eyes are drawn from the words to the city landscape that Gee alludes to.

Then it is back towards Lauris Edmond, passing Wellington born and bred Pat Lawlor on the way. Edmond sits on the busy city-to-sea bridge, and, suspended below here is poet, novelist, playwright, editor and scholar Vincent O'Sullivan. The bridge is itself a wonderful confusion of the work of Maori artist and carver Para Matchitt, stylized nikau palms and the floating steel ball sculpture of Neil Dawson. From here I can trace very easily where I have come from. It is only a few kilometres in distance. I have long lost any sense of time, such has been the delight in these encounters.

But I am in for one more surprise before I finish. Where is Denis Glover? The helpful guidebook to the Walk takes me to a waterside park. Still nothing. I continue to make the mistake of looking for the conventional. I should know better by now. I move to the water's edge so that I can look back to Te Papa and the Chaffers Marina. There he is, at my feet, apparently thrown up by some earlier storm and lodged in between the rocks, the evidence of his words right in front of me.

Denis Glover text sculpture 'Wellington Harbour is a Laundry'
Photo credit: Bruce Connew, Network Photographers

46

I was curious how the Society of Authors (PEN) committee went about realizing the vision of Dame Fiona Kidman, herself one of New Zealand's foremost writers. The committee made a list of possible writers to include and asked members of the Wellington Branch to rank them and make further suggestions. Eirlys Hunter who convened the committee says, 'We were always conscious that what we were doing was a beginning and we planned to add to it.'

The extracts were hard to choose and the inevitable pressures of time and money became issues. 'We asked the living writers for their suggestions,' says Hunter. 'We wanted to include a quote in Maori, from the oral tradition of a local iwi, but that proved too hard to pin down. It may happen in the future, in a collaboration with Te Papa. We shared the dead between us and read through the collected works and presented the other committee members with a choice ... We wanted contrast and to represent the writer's work fairly. We didn't want lots of ellipses and that meant that some of our favourite quotes wouldn't work as they were too long or too discursive or needed context.'

Hunter, like everyone I spoke to who was involved with this project, is enormously and justifiably pleased with the response from the people of Wellington and visitors. Hunter quotes from an e-mail from a teenager:

> *I was meaning to write just to tell you how great the waterfront poems are, it was lovely to only find them by accident when getting back and to have in words in front of me all the stuff I had missed about Wellington. I was walking with one of my friends who roller blades around there all the time and ain't your average poetry type and he was like 'yeah I know them all off by heart read them all the time, I think about all the different things they could mean*

This teenager is not the only one. It seems to me that immigrants are always searching for some sense of Arrival, as if waiting to be struck by lightning. It never quite happens like that or certainly not for this ex-Londoner. In the end, it becomes a matter of identity that is borne out by a variety of experiences. My time with these writers has been one such experience that confirms my sense of belonging to this city. I will go back.

Often.

Peter Farrell

LIVING HERE   Well you have to remember this place
is just one big city with 3 million people with
a little flock of sheep each so we're all sort of
shepherds
                little human centres each within an outer
circle of sheep around us like a ring of
covered wagons   we all know we'll probably
be safe when the Indians finally come
down from the hills   (comfortable to live
in the Safest Place in the World)
                                sheep being
very thick and made of wool and leather
being a very effective shield as ancient
soldiers would agree.
                And you can also
sit on them of course and wear them and eat them
so after all we are lucky to have these
sheep in abundance   they might
have been hedgehogs -
                Then we'd all be
used to hedgehogs and clothed in prickles
rather than fluff
                and the little sheep would
come out sometimes at night under the moon
and we'd leave them saucers of milk
                        and feel sad
seeing them squashed on the road
Well anyway here we are with all this
cushioning in the biggest city in the world
its suburbs strung out in a long line
and the civic centre at the bottom of
Cook Strait   some of them Hill Suburbs
and some Flat Suburbs and some more prosperous
than others
                some with a climate that embarrasses
them and a tendency to grow strange small fruit
some temperate and leafy   whose hot streets lull

So here we are again in the biggest
safest city in the world   all strung out
over 1500 miles one way   and a little bit
the other
        each in his woolly protection
so sometimes it's difficult to see out
the eyes   let alone call to each other
which is the reason for the loneliness some
of us feel
        and for our particular relations
with the landscape   that we trample
or stroke with our toes or eat or lick
tenderly or pull apart
                and love   like an
old familiar lover who fits us
curve to curve   and hate because it
knows us and knows our weakness
We're calling fiercely to each other
through the muffled spaces   grateful for
any wrist-brush
           cut of mind or touch of music,
lightning in the intimate weather of the soul.

Cilla McQueen

Mining

it begins being Cornish
pie pasty & stew twice a week
& no compulsion to eat vegetables

the rules are:
not too much noise or getting
in someone else's face
                    you can
do what you want, go to
the football & gigs, but no
regular money, just what can be
negotiated
            Father involved in
the unions & anti the monarchy
you grow up a secret royalist
& never join a union

FREEDOM has another face
can't be peeled away by the
hose on the clay, or blasted
to reveal itself
                slow digging
reaches it up &
the worms help, yes
you must have worms

a woman comes & tells you
what you're doing wrong, just like your mother

& when you're strong enough not to mind
everything gets easier
she helps you & then it doesn't matter
how long the digging takes

Owen Bullock

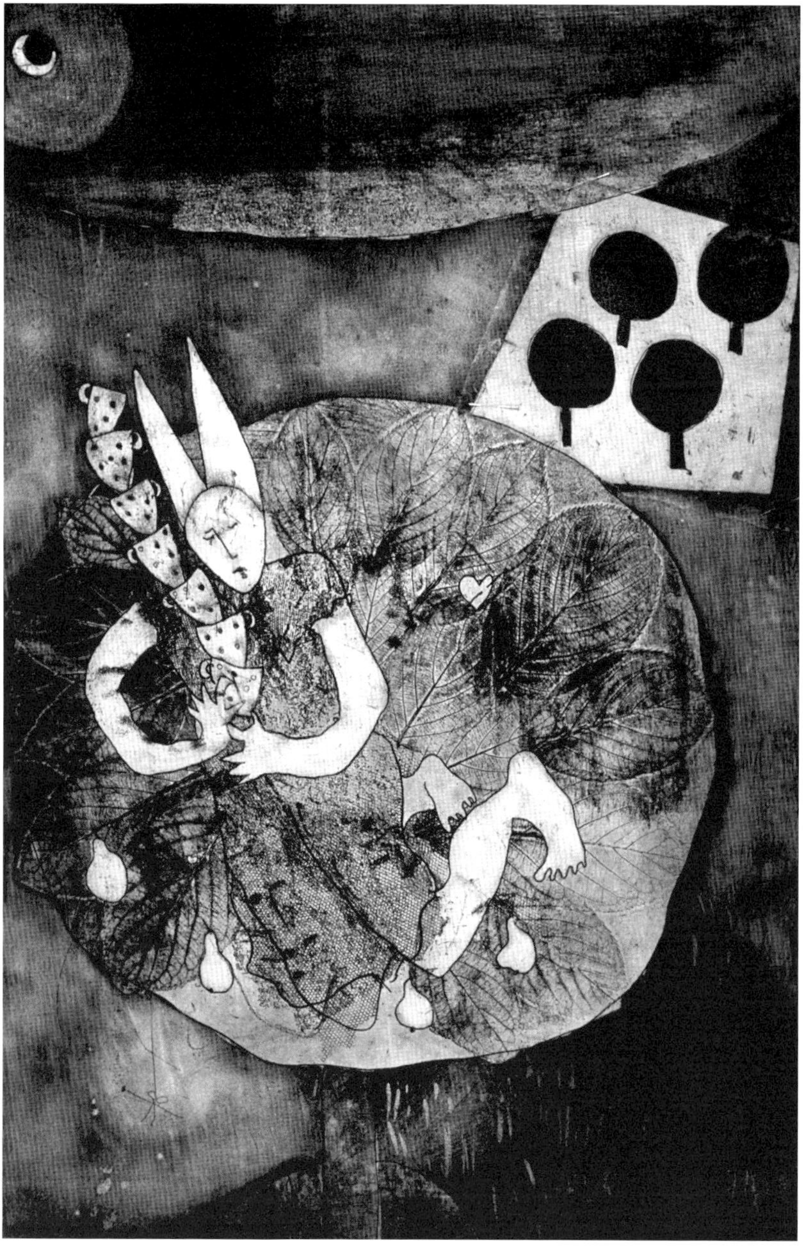

The Shark Callers

but I suddenly had no fear because the camera eroticizes the space!
                                            Spalding Gray

Men at their ease on the steps of the onestore
wives buy tinned fish with the sitdown money
men don't clock on down at the lagoon
women won't cook it children won't eat it
now they have tasted what money can buy
time to tease the man with the camera
tell him stories he wants to hear
hot wired to play cool they play it cool
the children dance the thrill of it all
- *The camera is looking at me!*

He's handholding a Hi-8 for broadcast quality this end of a tiny canoe.

A tiny canoe which is clinging to the blue heaving bosom of the ocean which is floating beneath the soaring blue arch of the dispassionate sky.

It's Steadicam of course so it rides the ocean like the man in the lens is riding the ocean side-saddle in his lap lap which he wears well letting the movement take him as if it is no movement his spine long and loose.

The camera is beside itself tense buttocks a locked spine it doesn't know what to expect but it wants to see it and to see it with broadcast quality.

- *Now watch this!* - says the man in the lap lap with a smooth intrusive glance he lifts a conch shell blows sweetly and longingly until the sound stains the sky drips into the sea - *Yeah yeah* - says the camera - *And?*

A shark breaks the water lifting his nose butting the side - *You called?*

The man who calls sharks leans tenderly into the water plunges his arms in up to the elbows takes hold of the shark who demurs writhes retreats so he may slap his tail against the resisting water and leap into the boat!

The camera goes - I *DO NOT BELIEVE WHAT I AM SEEING* - the man behind the camera remembers - *I must not drop the camera overboard!*

The camera starts seeing all over again
- *the achieve of, the mastery of the thing!*

The camera is lurking in a dusty corner of the meeting house.
His heartbeat slow he is breathing like a twitcher in his hide.

- *Yes yes* - says the Japanese trader talking shop - *I take these.
I pay dollars for these quality shark fin but I must have forty kilo.
It's not worth my skin unless you have forty kilo all at one time.*

The men from the lagoon with sub titles shuffle their feet.

- *We fast three days sleep apart from our wives and the fin is hung on the wall with all honour some men never have a shark fin hung the hero ancestor he had twenty hung forty kilo that would be - how many? - beyond imagining it is not in our contract with the shark they would not come we could not ask them to.*

The trader says with quick impatient movements - *Why won't they speak to me? I'm going crazy trying to get sense out of these stone age guys they can't deliver. If only I could be back at head office pushing a button to see the monthly figures.*

The camera says - *IT'S ALL MAGIC IT'S ALL MAGIC ANYWAY.*
The camera says - *SPEAK TO ME I SMILE AT EVERYTHING.*

Jennifer Compton

The Weight Of Cows

Cows are impossibly heavy,
they are the dark matter
that astrophysicists talk of.
All the weight of the universe
can be accounted for, if
you include cows.

It is this weight that splays
hooves, deep into the mud,
draws milk down to bursting
udders, makes cow pats slap
the earth with uncanny force.

Even milked-out
they move heavily. Arching
knuckled backs under the sting
of the auctioneer's stick, they buckle
and stagger as if their very bones
are recast from bedsteads
or rusted park railings.

To see a cow hoisted
into the air by one hind leg
is to witness
the death of a planet.

Mandy Coe

THE CHOCOLATE POLISHER

Last in the line
of dollopers and makers, I create
the unblemished sheen revealed
as each lid is lifted
with a slow rustling yawn.

I bring about the illusion, wipe
away clues of anonymous haste:
screaming clank and heat;
the sickly-sweet air that clings
to our clothes. All fingerprints

are erased with my quick
white gloves, my soft cloth.
Lift, wipe Lift, wipe. Every chocolate
laid to rest in the dark, innocent
as a closed eye.

I picture a woman, the open box
resting in her lap.
Her fingers hover as she decides.
It is proof of my skill: that trust,
her belief in this perfect hush.

Mandy Coe

DOULTON LADY

You were always there
when I stayed with her, during the war.
When I was frightened she brought you
from the beige tiled mantlepiece,
into the room where I slept.
You were my guardian Granny,
gazing down from a tall shelf.
I dozed in the warm drift of your red shawl
that fell in a 'V' down the length of your back.

Today, on a visit years later,
I filch you from the cabinet,
hold you in my palm.

You are gesture moulded in china:
long skirts flow in porcelain folds,
your small pink hands twitch your gown up
to show a froth of petticoats, a painted shoe.
Your shawl is glazed with a sweet crush
of cranberries, plums. Under a broad bonnet
your lips glow in a damson simper.
Remnants of something fragile shatter
as I hold you in my hands.

Jill Eulalie Dawson

ALCHEMY   the shock is that we met as usual
for Nescafé in the arcade. a plastic table
among muzaq and the concrete rumble of skateboards
and we talked of nothing much
- afterwards I try to make them believe this.

it is only as you turned to wave I saw it briefly
- your plastic ignition key - bright yellow
as you would soon be in your cloak
of petro fumes, eyes open (they tell me)
to the screams of Thursday morning shoppers.

I didn't spot it, mind already in Morrisons.
you had even pulled our table,
juddering over studs of gum,
away from that earnestly puffing family, and now,
branded on my retina, that yellow lighter.

Char March

CITY OF STRANGERS

The door opens
And his face eases
Like a man who has forgotten
Everything.

The rumbling concerto
Of voices, how a woman peels
A coat from her
Speckled shoulders.

What holds us here —
The shattered mosaic
Of reflections,
The last dirty kiss

While winter kicks its feet
Outside.

David Ford

ECHOES

Go early, as I do,
abandon your car
on th lower slopes
and let the mist
wrap around you
as you stride out
towards the clouds.

At the summit
stop and turn,
watch the yellow lights
from the town
slowly switch on the day.

Then cup your hands,
shout out all those things
you've always wanted to say,
and wait for the mountains
to bounce your defiance to the world.

Idris Caffrey

MATTERHORN I
Surely he must be
One of God's fingers

Declining us
For the millionth time,

A signal, a warning,
Pointing at men.

II
They came in 1863
To this magnet:

Three Oxford graduates,
A parson from Lincolnshire,

Now their graves wear
Plastic flowers.

III
And still he waits
High above judgment

Demanding
New hostages

In his great solitude
Spending desire.

Lotte Kramer

BOY: 'I had no say in it.
They plucked me by my hair
Out of the crowd
And rushed me to the hospital.

I knew no one.
Had seen my father shot,
My mother beaten, chased away,
I ran and ran into the night
With shooting deafening the air.

I found a cave to hid in,
Cold, alone, and slept a while.
At dawn I stumbled out
Looking for people, food,

And joined a group of children
Like myself, abandoned,
Wounded, stealing
Where we could
From empty houses.

The road was sandy, hot,
We swallowed dust and thirst,
But then it led us to the border
And to many hands.'

Lotte Kramer

NIGERIA HIGH COMMISSION De Nigeria High Commission
Dem hol' demsef in high opinion.
Dem treat you like de labour unions,
Dem no care for your opinions.

If you call dem for fone
Forever you get engaged tone.
Dem vex u in your bone
An u be no alone.

De other day I call dem for fone, I manage get thru.
De woman sey 'Hello, what can I do for you?'
I say 'I wan put ma son for ma passport'
She say 'come with your forms and £37 postal order'.

When I get dere I show ma form and postal order
Dem tell me 'something is not quite in order'
I ask 'wetin wrong ma brotha'
Him seh 'u need letter from the mother!'
'But de woman on de fone said...'
'Don't worry what de woman said,
I'm telling you what the boss said'.
'But oga I've come from far away...'
'You go, come back another day'.
'But oga I no live in London...'
'Are you deaf or are you a moron!!??'

So I go, come back another day
On the train I get very long delay.
I get form, postal order and letter from mother.
Ah beg ooo this time nothing go be out of order.

When I get dere I be a bit late
I been travelling since a quarter to eight.
Dis long queue, wetin I go do?
Up dere in front, dere's much ado.
Some woman don make the cashier man come vex
'Position closed' he don leave for his Porsche Corvette.
Who go take our forms and postal order?
We come start ask and look at one another.
'Come back tomorrow...' the other man start to explain.
'Abasi mbok ooo' dis no deh happen again.

Nigeria High Commission, u be disgrace to our nation.
Nigeria High Commission, u need proper education.
Nigeria High Commission, mek u learn from other nations.
Nigeria High Commission, mek u do am for our nation.

Ugbana Oyet

YORKSHIRE OPEN POETRY COMPETITION

1st. Prize £500, 2nd. £250, 3rd. £100,
Yorkshire Prize £50, 10 further prizes.
Adjudicator: Kevin Crossley-Holland   Closing Date: August 10th

Line limit of 80 lines. Entry fee: £3.50 per poem or £12.00 for four. No entry form required. Send entries and/or for a copy of the rules to: YOPC 2003, 32, Spey Bank, Acomb Park, York YO24 2UZ (must be accompanied by SAE).

For further information about a day poetry events in York on November 8th send SAE to: YOPC 2003, The Old Dairy, Malton Street, Coulton, Nr. Hovingham YO62 4NE.

My Friend Est

My fricnd Est, she got curly black hair
She pretty as a princess, her eyes like ebony
Her skin is ivory, I like her anatomy
Call he on d fone, I ask her come dine with me.

My friend Est, we know she d best
With her gentle caress, she drives away my stress
Takes the worries off my chest
May she Jah bless.

My friend Est, together we smoke an drink
Been together so long, she knows what I think
She even feel how I feel
To her, my tears I reveal.

My friend Est, she so kind an sweet
Like to shake her kundi to d beat
As she walk down our street
An drink her vodka neat.

My friend Est, she like dynamite
She dey make me laugh all nite
As we watch the Mike Tyson fight
Jah say everything gonna be awright.

My friend Est, she love her Irish Meadow
After a few bottles we all feelin mellow
We drink with Flash, dat crazy blonde fellow
I'll be gone now, but will come back tomorrow.

Ugbana Oyet

Duncan's Dream

One night when Duncan went to bed he dreamt of nothing but cats in the strangest places. On waking he felt so uneasy that he decided to look up the dreambook to see if he could work out what it meant. The book said that dreaming of cats was an extremely unfortunate omen and indicated treachery from someone the dreamer loved or trusted.

Duncan racked his brains to think of the person the dream might be referring to. He thought of all the people he was closest to and which one was the most likely to betray him. He tossed the idea around in his head for several hours trying to remember which one of his friends he had spoken to last and if they had behaved in any strange or unusual way. Had they done something out of character that was suspicious, or had any of them any reason to deceive him? He considered every person he could think of, including his girlfriend Susie whom he worked with, until he was totally depressed and worn out with it all. He went to work in what psychologists might refer to as an acutely paranoid state, whereby he was careful about everything he said and did and kept one eye on his back all day. He wondered, as he opened his mail, whether he would ever be able to trust anyone again.

When he got home from work, after pouring himself a stiff drink he went straight for the Tarot cards. He got a reversed High Priestess crossed by the Tower. He knew that this meant he wasn't listening to what his intuition was telling him and there was some sort of drastic change on its way. He hadn't been doing the cards long so his interpretation was rather vague.

That night he dreamt the same dream again. The cats this time were larger with more fur and had far more of an attitude. He woke up sweating with palpitations. He tried his hand at the I Ching to see if that would shed light on his dream interpretation and on the situation generally. The hexagram that he got was one that advised him to do away with the old and start something new. He couldn't make out what it was referring to exactly so the following day he did it again. But he still wasn't any clearer. Before he knew it he was throwing the coins every day. If he had an angry conversation on the phone with one of his customers, he threw the coins to find out why. If the washing machine flooded and he couldn't get anyone in to fix it, out would come the coins or the cards, or on particularly bad days, he would do both. How could he possibly know the reason for any trouble or joy without consulting the oracle?

He began a routine where he threw the coins every morning while he ate his bacon and egg. If he had time he took notes on what it said on a piece of paper which, he carried with him to Scottish Widows.

At teabreak when he scooted outside for a Silk Cut or at lunchtime in the canteen, he unfolded his paper to remind him what kind of day he was supposed to be having. If for some obscure reason he hadn't had enough time in the morning to throw the coins, he would smoke double his normal amount, drink twice as much coffee and generally spend the whole day in a state of acute anxiety, unable to concentrate on any of his filing or urgent insurance claims.

One Monday in June before he went to work he did the I Ching as usual and came up with a hexagram whose message was to avoid 'putting new wine into old bottles.' The implications were that drastic change was indicated and the situation was about to transform itself irretrievably. It stated very clearly that there was 'no longer any place in his life for anything which didn't serve his best interests.' He wondered whether this might relate to his relationship with Susie which for the past two years had been in serious stagnation. He pondered all day at work what the hexagram was referring to. At lunch time he sneaked off to the park and did the Tarot to see if that would make it clearer. Once again the High Priestess was there in all her glory but reversed and crossed by the Devil. He interpreted this as a very old habit pertaining to his lower drives which was blocking his intuition. He spent another night tossing and turning trying to decide what action needed to be taken. The next morning he fried his bacon and thought carefully. He was worried that if he didn't take action quickly, his opportunity for a new life would pass him by. He went back to work resigned to break up with his childhood sweetheart as he was sure that was what the cards and the I Ching were trying to tell him. Susie couldn't believe her ears when he sat down with her at the afternoon coffee break they both shared and told her his decision.

'But what have I done wrong,' she asked him in disbelief?'

'You haven't done anything wrong,' he reassured her, 'it's just that this is the decision I've come to.' He offered her no further explanation, even though she was devastated and had to be taken back to her desk by a colleague. The poor girl couldn't work out how the man she thought she was going to marry had suddenly dumped her for no apparent reason.

Duncan felt immensely relieved that evening after breaking the news to Susie. He most definitely felt that it was the right thing for him to do.

Now he could look forward to a life of challenges and risks. But then, about ten minutes after his Chinese take away arrived and he was eating it alone, he started to worry that perhaps he had been a little hasty about breaking up with her. What if another Tarot book could have offered him a different interpretation with less drastic consequences? He wasn't sure.

His throat dried up and he began to panic. He put the Chinese meal to one side and pulled out a set of rune stones. He chose several from their velvet pouch, but he couldn't make head nor tail of their meaning and threw them on the floor in exasperation.

The next day at work his stomach churned all day. He avoided the canteen even for a coffee in case he bumped into his ex.

At last he was released from the office but going home felt uncomfortable and he couldn't get rid of the feeling that he'd done something terribly wrong.

However as the days passed he began to feel as if he had made the right decision and although it had been hard at the beginning it was actually the best course of action he could have taken. His heart hardened. The soft spot that he once carried around with him was there no longer. He bought a different style of clothes, suits from Austin Reed, shirts from Van Heusen and his sale bargains from Burtons went in the bin. He no longer flinched when he saw Susie in the other office, she was like a distant memory that no longer concerned him. He eyed up a different kind of woman. The kind that would have previously eaten him for breakfast, the kind that two months ago he would have been scared to say hello to. He looked stronger and more confident. He put in for promotion. He was the obvious candidate with the most relevant experience. He went for an interview which he thought went well. He was self assured, confident in his new self image and articulate as a public schoolboy. But he didn't get it. This troubled him. He couldn't understand why he'd been knocked back. His new found confidence wavered. Who else could have got it? He asked around the office, but no one seemed to know anything about it. Promotion meant a substantial increase in pay, a higher grade, considerable authority. Who could it be? Definitely someone who was well in with management, who was in the know and could have put the boot in.

As he was having his mid morning coffee and reading the paper, in walked Susie with a pale pink suit, a briefcase under her arm, tweaking a loose hair on her upper lip.

67

She stood looking at her watch like the cat who'd got the cream.
'I think Mr Anderson, she said, 'it's time you were back at work. Your tea break ended five minutes ago.'

She waltzed off clicking her new high heels and wiggling her bottom down the corridor. Duncan who had not expected this turn of events in the least went back to his desk fuming. Much later that evening when he had taken another of his hot patchouli baths, he began to realise exactly what his dreams of the cats had been trying to tell him. Like a man condemned he pulled out the deck and laid out another spread.

Mandy MacFarlane

Sun Café Writers

Join Friends of the Sun Café!

✳ *Free admission to Café events*
✳ *Discount on* **Dream Catcher**
✳ *Local author's work for sale*
✳ *Open 7 days per week*
✳ *Room hire for events*
✳ *Internet Access (£1 per hour)*
✳ *Video Conference (£2 per hour)*

7 St Mary's Street, Lincoln
opposite the railway station

For application forms to join **Friends of the Sun Café** contact the café telephone 01522 579067

F817GFE

You must have loved me
to let me do that; I must
have loved you to want to,
in Saltburn-by-the-Sea-
we-never-saw, remember?

Tonight I saw you trembling
expectantly at the lights,
some big-handed stranger
at the wheel and the song
of that old engine calling.

Shower curtains of ripe leaves,
blue dolphin soap
I won't forget, and those places
language lurches towards
but never reaches.

Strange how the past crumps
and crimples itself for storage,
cerebrum rolled out, folded in
like pastry, only to rise torrid
and descant with surprise.

We must have been in love,
for want of a better word,
a word that no one has used
before, ever; or since,
in Saltburn-by-the-Sea.

Round the clock together,
motorways, byways, lay-bys,
all weathers. Off she goes,
dragging six good years
and 100,000 miles
of me behind her.

Sam Gardiner

DEAR YOU

Delighted to have daylight to see you by
as night to not, to watch you taking shape
from inside out in labial pink and cherry,
composing your risen self in silksoft lamina,
blue on blue, leaf smoke on sky. And then,

dear you, making leary mouths in the glass
and spending ages on the face that ages
before you. Had I been myself I could have
told you you weren't yours, in that lipstickless
self-portrait in reverse, the mirror's invention.

I can write it now you're gone, have left me
my self again (I tell myself) alone with words
in a room. Poetry is for those who need it,
you say, who don't, defining the heart's need,
provoking love-notes you will never read.

Sam Gardiner

None of His Own

He rings to hear our TV in the background,
having none of his own,
and my wife

(having none of his own)
coaching me above the din
to invite him round for a few drinks or two

in the warmth of our
over-insured but suddenly unsubstantial
family home,

and long kisses in our
newly fitted, forever dreamed-of kitchen,
having none of his own,

while I tidy away the children
and read them electrifying bedtime stories
he keeps buying specially,

and try to invent
lawful reasons for borrowing his chain-saw,
having none of my own.

Sam Gardiner

The New Kimono

Hilda slipped it on, wrapped it round herself,
her eyes dazzled delighted
she stroked the satin stalks scattered
over the gown,
they flashed silver against
the slate blue of the background.
She looked in the mirror,
her dark straight hair and tiny frame
she could pass for a geisha
Hilda took minute steps to make the
point to herself.
'Would you like me to serve you tea?'
she bowed to Sam and set the tray
with best china. Sam smiled.
'Is that an appropriate exchange?'
He was shy to suggest anything else,
'Tea will be fine' he said.
Hilda moved to the kitchen
he followed
'Have you missed me?'
'Of course,' she said, turned and
kissed him.
He locked her in his arms.
As she put her arms up round his neck,
the kimono opened revealing her
nakedness, he swallowed approvingly
slid his hand down her belly to the
soft mass of hair.
'Oh I have missed that too,' she said,
picked up the kimono, flew upstairs
she hung it on a hanger behind the door,
yes that is lovely, she thought,
grabbed some perfume, rubbed it on
her arms, picked up her old kimono
She said to herself,
'I'll give it to the girls to dress up in.
That will keep them occupied for a while.'

Gloria Grove-Stephensen.

SUDDENLY STREET LIGHTS
for Eleanor Wilner

On that throaty crow-call at the end of day
you notice such things as ravaged corn-husks
and ragwort losing colour to rough shade.

Then a hum comes when ground shapes blend
where you and the earth meld, brokenly,
while birds threading clouds perform a sketch of sky.

When, wrapped in their giant leaves, two dying sunflowers
hunched over, seem weary, heavily-cloaked travellers
trudging out of Walsingham into the spelled gloom,

You close the patio doors, draw the drapes,
put the garbage out, turn in and wait:
there is much to ripen in the warm, dark night.

Lucy Brennan

SEPTEMBER DYING

I've come in
and left the leaves
where split light lances.

I've come in
and left the stones
to the dew.

I've come in
for wherever I move
a dark shadow dances.

I've come in
as whispering night
claims its due.

I've come in
now that sight can't curve
on the swallow swooping.

I've come in
with the weight of death
in my head.

I've come in
for the air's turned cold,
and an owl is hooting.

I've come in
but the door's only glass
and sunset's come through in red.

Lucy Brennan

THE AUDITION

The janitor's metal bucket clanks
in the corridor. On dark wood
my shoes are pink lipstick blotted with chalk.
Unbinding the tight ribbons,
my blue fingertips shake,
whilst the bruised glass of my feet
holds the used music quiet.
Outside the night pulls indigo silk
over the high windows. I see myself prise
the long fingers of flowers from my hair.
He'll wash the floor now.
I take my pink shoes and run.

Elizabeth Stott

THE SAND-TIMER
IN MEMORY OF JULIET SWAIN

It was kept in the kitchen to time eggs
Though it never served its proper purpose:
Being too bulky, and on its last legs;
Yet curved curvaceously, with a cool poise.
A familiar family heirloom
Passed from mother to daughter down the line
Now done and dusted in an empty room.
How I love the way it balances between
The arm; the sand at top trickling toward
A point no bigger than the prick of a pin:
Then the slow grow; grains coming up clean;
The sifted sands of time slowly gathered —
Like watching rings ripple from a cast stone:
Each ellipse eclipsed, dissolved down to one.

R.J.Stallon

NYMPHOMANIAC   That morning before you woke,
I climbed the hundred steps to the attic floor
and curled on the window-seat
outside the nymphomaniac's flat.

She didn't know me from Adam,
but I swore once she read the simple note
I slipped under her door, telling how
I'd just spent the whole night

with my back turned to you in the next bed,
listening to you with a stranger,
- the sudden hisses and drawn out sighs,
the strange silences between, -

she'd smile and make an allowance
for my virginity. Welcome me
into the milk-white dressing gown
they said she always answered in.

Slowly lift the latch between us
like the click of a music box
playing *Suzanne*, the three *Gnossiennes,*
or *Let No Man Steal Your Thyme.*

Below me in the courtyard
a statue turned imperceptibly on its plinth.
Coppiced plane trees numb with frost
pulled on fingerless gloves.

Already birds were gathering
in the gauzy quiet dawn,
over the battlefields of gardens and yards;
wild geese that had lost their way,

nightingales that sang out of tune,
seagulls embarrassed by their size,
solitary magpies, burnt-out robins, whip birds,
and kingfishers afraid to dive.

Dozens more I didn't recognise,
shivering as the city stretched and stirred.
All waiting on that narrow window-ledge
for the nymphomaniac to wake.

Mark Czanik

WITNESS I still hear her
crying
that banging and crashing

then nothing.

38 minutes past 7:
finished watching the news.
Made a cup of tea.

Tracy was crying
Lisa was clumping about
packing bags.

I didn't see him
come in
but I heard him
go up
heard the noise of him
shouting
where the hell are you
going

then the crack
something breaking.

Then nothing.

She should've been
crying - I just
wanted to hear her.

Now the banging and
yelling goes on
in my head

and what the coroner said

and the doctor who say
it's just tinnitus

and I can't go by
that room
without knowing

and in the dark
all I see is
the stain on the wallpaper

growing.

André Mangeot

AFTER EIGHT On her way back from the library exchanging Mill's book -
& what a boon for the twee librarian with a stamper -
she had Bach on the walkman:
Singet as down alleys, ranging
platoons of the scum of the place
scrawled with a tile cutter
blagged from the D.I.Y.
City Suck Cock on the plate
glass of the medical centre's face;
scored.

Jed kicked in the Scottie,
dog shit splattered his trainers
and he wheeled and spat
abusive in short words
(he had a limitled vocabulary,
excluded since year six) at Minnie.

She turned up the volume, sucked
chocolate covered mints and stared
straight-wise into a closed-up Boots.
You: fucker!
(pulse is adrenaline pumped at this point)
the dog is in fits from its kicking
the chemist has hidden behind rows
of Mum which he keeps
stocked up and in front in case as Jed
turns on her face in fixations of terror
as he gets his kicks from the only power he's shafted
off from life, this fixing
of scaring the shits out of women.

He doesn't always bring the knife, tonight
for example he just used up his ammo' of fists
turned Bach on the Walkman to small

electronic components in the gutter
Mill's to shredded paper fluttered
offwise in the wind that howls
down and through the open malls.
No one gave a fuck.

She was left as a mess in the doorway
He was as ever,
a Scot:
free.

Emma-Jane Arkady

After the Hurricane

I take a camera-eye view:
drunken pool, smashed seawall,
thatch palms stunned
under an uncomfortable sun,
mindless as this blue morning,
this salt-sodden shore.

Soon I will make love
to a beautiful memory
in a blind-darkened room.
I will lose the light
and find passion?
Grief? Heartbroken

after the hurricane, after
the mourning is done,
like the sky, like
the sea,
I will be still
here.

K.V. Skene

VIOLON D'INGRES
AFTER A PHOTOGRAPH BY MAN RAY

Two perfect soundholes — one sloping
and one backward S — traced on his lover's back
turn her into a shapely violin. It seems surreal
just like the fur lined cup and saucer
the telephone complete with lobster handset.

Until the night at the concert
when I watch the pain
of the man whose double bass
is alive from scroll to spike
as he hugs her slim waist to him.

And those cries from the depths
of her brown belly
are growing urgent as he reaches down
to pluck the higher notes.

Kathryn Daszkiewicz

HOT LOVE

In '72 he was my main man. My ear glued
to a cheap transistor as the double decker lurched
through glitterless suburbs to the comprehensive.

I'd carve his name in every desk I sat in -
a point of honour. Head full of lyrics to add mystery
to Mrs Rapley's slides of igneous rocks.

A tube of eye-shadow from Woolworths
purple — his favourite colour (so it said in *Jackie*)
for the night he jumped from a star at City Hall

and older girls threw knickers on the stage. I thought
I might faint as I waved my scarf and screamed
with less flat chested children of the revolution.

I stuck with him through the vodka and the pills.
Bought *Popswap, Music Star* - to trade the toothy Osmonds
the Jackson 5 or David Cassidy for his now rarer face.

He left me dreaming of that local boy who sprayed
MARC BOLAN LIVES on a gable end and then ran off
to say goodbye, see for himself the white swan made of flowers.

Kathryn Daszkiewicz

LETTER TO WILGEFORTIS

In a time of steeds she'd have placed
a peck of oats, as was the custom,
at the base of your statue.

She would have known your story
well. Instead, she chances on it:
a double-take at the plate of a bearded lady
in some musty hagiography.

You'd caught the fancy of a pagan king,
begged god to make you unattractive.
That heaven-sent moustache made
your suitor bristle. And your flesh father
had you promptly crucified.

Your other names — Uncumber, Liberata,
hint at your specialism: spouse disposal.
Well, husbands, anyway. She wonders if
you still oblige? If so, what should she offer
in this day and age? A can of petrol —
he could ride to the devil, even now.
Or will oats still suffice? You rig a race;
he legs it with some blonde.

I know she'll give
whatever it takes
to make that killing distance —
that started somehow, when she wasn't looking —
both physical and permanent.

Kathryn Daszkiewicz

NO DEMAND   Her local florist says there's no demand
for dahlias around these parts -

he's got chrysanths, carnations, gyp,
got freesias, roses, (salesmanship)

but dahlias - *A Peace Pact, Easter Sunday,
Silver City* - not a chance. There's no demand.

Picture his surprise, then,
when she points a stubby finger in his face,

the stubby finger of an outraged housewife
in a state of shock

that life has pitched her up some place
where pompous round and soft

as ladies' 1960s bathing-caps,
aren't loved, aren't worshipped -

worse, aren't even kept in stock.
Picture his discomfort when,

amid the curling ribbons, sheets of cellophane
and rustic paraphernalia,

amid the alien lilies, *Get Well* cards,
the pale pink roses, white azaleas,

she tells him *she* demands
- and quick -

a glorious, gaudy, tasteless, raucous, non-U
lorryload (make that a juggernaut) of dahlias.

Jenny Swann

THINKING OF BENNY

Willie Nelson singing *Always On My Mind*
like he was old enough to mean it,
Hank recalling a lifetime of godless last rites,
and the day Benny Jacobs the gofer
stood like an ox the other side
of his giant desk, the odd finger
on his proletarian fist missing
as usual, but crying this time, maudlin drunk
I've just learnt my wife's
planning to bury me Jewish

they'd done Hilter and Stalin together,
him and Naomi, days when the Party
ran out of cards, but ways must part
and the last shred of rational praxis
was vanishing into Benny's mist;
what was he supposed to say to make it better?
Benny liked to hear him lay down the line,
a bedtime story with tank tracks
so you're not a complete fool, then, Hank?
but there was no line on the marital hereafter

now Benny's a ghost;
Hank wasn't there for the passing,
he doesn't go to funerals so much these days,
the red tie gathers dust in the wardrobe;
Willie's finished, and he finds he's humming
the words of a crazy old song
          higher and higher and higher
          we'll follow the Soviet star
falling over New York Street,
crumpling into Quarry Hill Flats

Gordon Wardman

Photos

ileh, my twin
I speak with you now
in another tongue

these pictures you gave me
sit in my still house
whilst I wander
the cafes of this
well-trodden town

these pictures you sent me
say —
say how much ileh,
my twin, my loved one
you struggle

for all I see
is the brown photo
the layer on layer
on layer of

a moment of time

time which is gone
discarded

the silk finish of the image
meets my gaze
its handing over
by our mother
the only moment which
touches me

she hands these brown photos
over with her mottled hands

as mine begin, in turn
to mottle too.

my insides ache
for another world

I see a dolly, a mannequin
- a moment of pleasure
- of one being held in adoration

scalloped dress
- who made it?
who held needle to
fabric
who lost their eyes
to make the silk dress
sit so pretty on those
knees?

uniform. Coquette
elegance as a gift,
not acquired.

do not pry into these moments
I am happy with the picture
of her sweet legs
crossed the last time I saw her
her blue eyes
twinkling over her goodlife
over her pleasures
over her
power.

Julia Davis

Driving Through Jerusalem

I'd not planned
on driving
through Jerusalem,

had intended
to pull into a layby
and there swap places
with you.

Too late I realised
I'd missed the last exit.

'Hold my hand!'
I pleaded,
panic-stricken.

'I think you might need it
to drive with,'
you replied,

taking it all the same,
keeping hold
as we stopped,
started,
accelerated too,
all in second gear.

No matter now
the convoy of car horns
crawling behind us.

'They can wait,'
you said,
making me laugh.

Less easy to laugh now
you've let go
not just of my hand
but of me as well.

I'd not planned
on driving through life
with the passenger seat
always empty.

Ruth Beckett

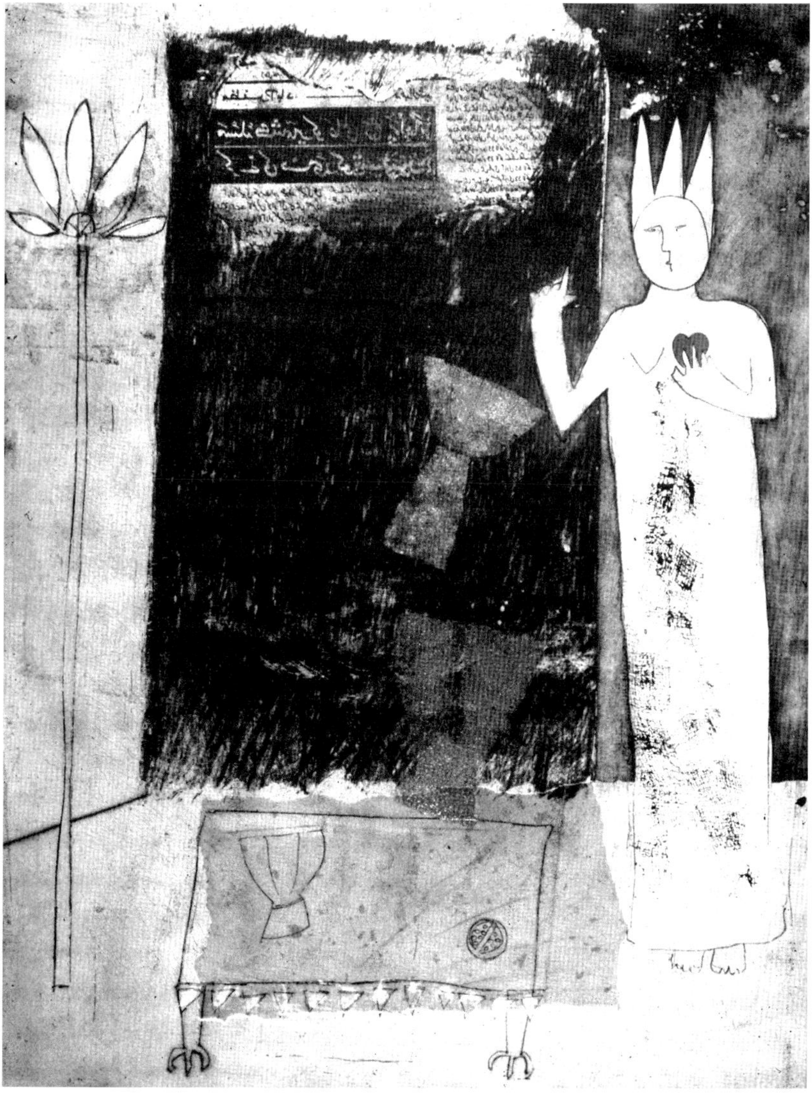

Impossible Lake

Once there lived a woman named Fullay Lahara.

That means Fullay The Deep in our tongue, though she was known by other names. Fullay Fierce Eye some called her, for her eyes were sunken like two deep, black pools, and even the strongest of men dared not stare into them for too long. In the last years of her life, she was known as Fullay The Grim. A sinewy limbed, leathery skinned woman, her stern face was cracked and lined with the scars of age. People of the Noatun district feared and respected her. She had knowledge of healing and, some said, the power to weave a curse. People shrank from her bright stare and her harsh tongue, and being a woman of great intelligence she had little time for the small, mean minds of most of the dwellers in Noatun.

Fullay was also a great dreamer, a reader of dreams, and one night she had a powerful, important dream of her own. The dream told Fullay to exchange the sun for seven stars, the moon for six. She was shown where to dig a pit in the earth. This pit she was asked to fill with water and into the water she had to cast her thirteen stars. From those stars there would spiral open a whole fiery, glistening galaxy. Each new star would explode to become a beautiful flower, the flowers would transform into new-born children, and these children would be healthy, happy and would live long, fruitful lives.

Fullay awoke with the awareness that her dream had been of great significance.

Wise in the symbols of dreams, after a morning's contemplation she understood her dream well enough. The message of the dream set an excitement smouldering in her stomach, and over the poor evening meal she told Tyre, her husband, of her inspired plan.

Tyre shook his head grimly at her wild ideas. He was a stocky, practical man who had been a miner in the days of the mine. Since losing his right hand in an accident at the mine, he had been of no use to any employer. Now he put his strength into helping Fullay work the land, but even with his help they were only just managing to scrape a living from the fields around their dwelling. Even though he saw a glimmer of sense and logic in his wife's plan he thought that her idea was too ambitious to work in reality. Her plan though was simple enough to say:

'I'm going to make a lake. Dig one. Fill it with water and fish. Listen, here's my plan...' She went on, and he listened. When she had finished speaking Tyre mulled over her words a while, staring at his spoon.

'There's no way,' he eventually said. 'There's no time. The work involved, for a start. And there'd never be enough water. Not from one stream. And the fish. What would you do about fish in this desert?'

'Ways can be found,' she answered, trying to keep a calm edge in her voice. 'Fish can be bought, and the lake is nothing but a matter of hard work. I can do that. I'm surprised that no one thought of it before.'

He continued to shake his head but she pressed him with reasons, with plans, even sketching her ideas with her finger on the table top between them. After an hour of this talk Tyre shrugged mutely. He had given in, knowing that she meant what she was saying. For Fullay the idea was no vague, half-formed scheme. Her dream had signalled a certainty. Even as she sat there she knew where, and how, to get her fish.

'All I ask from you is to stand by me with this,' she said, reaching over the table, tenderly resting her hand upon his arm.

'I'll be jeered and called a crazy woman, that's for sure. But I'll work on the lake in the morning, and in the afternoon I'll be here to help you. It'll tire me I know, but it won't be forever.'

And so it was settled between the two of them that she would go ahead with her plan.

Fullay put her idea before a meeting of the village council but as she had expected was ridiculed and laughed at for her trouble. Absurd, they said. Insane. Unworkable. Even when she approached neighbours, including women who like herself had lost children to disease and malnutrition, she was met with the same sneering ridicule. Yet in her heart she knew that if she could meet the conditions of her dream then her plan would work. She was so certain that one morning, a week after putting her idea before the village council, she took a barrow, a pick and a shovel up the hill behind Noatun, making her way to the spring that was the source of the districts only untainted water. There she spat on her callused hands, rubbed them together, and took up her pick axe.

Her work upon the impossible lake had begun.

Fullay's plan was simple and noble. She wanted to change the fortunes of Noatun by providing a food source that was nutritious and plentiful. The district had once been a mining area, its ramshackle village having been scrambled up at the heart of a sprawl of open cast quarries, pits and mineworkings. The coal and minerals ripped from the earth there had not been plentiful. Once the ground had been plundered, the mines no longer profitable, the company had closed down its works and moved away, taking employment and any real source of money with it. The works were now derelict, the narrow road that the company had built for its trucks broken and sprouting weeds. The whole district was quite arid, the soil barren, gritty dust, and but for the mines there would never have been a sensible reason for humans to settle there. With the soils capable of supporting only wilted grain crops and sinewy root vegetables, the people suffered badly after the closure of the mines, surviving only by scratching a food supply from that begrudging land. Some years whole crops had failed and vegetables had rotted in the earth with disease, causing hunger and malnutrition throughout the district, many of the children and the elderly perishing to sickness and starvation.

What Fullay had seen in the symbols of her dream was the creation of a fresh water lake at the heart of the district. A lake stocked with healthy, edible fish, surrounded by fertile, terraced gardens where fruit trees blossomed and patches of healthy vegetables thrived.

'It will work,' Fullay insisted when trying to press her neighbours to help her with the scheme. 'Just look around you. The holes in the earth. Those quarries there. Can't you see them, filled with water?'

But nobody else could see, and so for months Fullay continued to work alone, hacking and digging into the dusty earth. There was a suitable quarry, shallow and hard rocked, just to the east of the village itself. Fullay had seen that if a trench could be dug from the spring in the hills to this quarry, and then back from the quarry to the natural course of the stream, then her lake could easily be conceived. Work. Hard work.

That's all that was needed to create a hole filled with water. So simple really.

And the fish?

Well, they were another matter.

A sun and a moon for thirteen stars.

Only Fullay herself understood the answer to that cruel riddle.

Every morning Fullay went into the hills to work on her trench. From the bubbling pool where the spring of water emerged she began to hack and shovel a deep, narrow ditch which she lined with flat stones from a nearby quarry. Beneath the harsh morning sun it was hard, hot work, hands blistering, back and limbs growing sore with the labour, but she cared little for such suffering. To live to see blossoming, well fed faces of children in the green shade of trees around her fertile lake - that alone would be reward enough for her toils and pain.

After a morning's labour on the ditch, followed by an afternoon helping her husband tend their own dusty gardens, Fullay would eat the simple meal that Tyre had prepared for them. Come bed time she was exhausted and would fall into a deep, dreamless sleep. Fullay the Dream Reader, too busy and tired with her labours to even dream herself now. Yet slowly, hour by hour, her single important dream carved itself into reality upon the landscape of Noatun.

Many of Fullay's neighbours were amazed and inspired by her dedication to the work upon the ditch, and most ceased in their ridiculing of her. Seeing the trench slowly scratched out toward the quarry at the edge of the village, and realising the practicality of having fresh water so close at hand, some other women from the district began to turn up in a morning with shovels and pick-axes, ready now to help her with the task. With this help the trench to the quarry was soon completed. Earth and stones were heaped around the rim to damn the lower end of the quarry. Terraces for planting were shaped and cleared of boulders. Shrubs and tree saplings were planted around the quarry so that their roots could bind together the loose, dusty soil. Noatun had not seen such hard work and industry since the mining company had arrived there many years before.

Work of digging out the second trench began, a trench from the village side of the quarry back into the course of the stream. The earth here was iron-hard. Work was backbreaking and slow for even the strongest of the diggers, and the frustrations were many. And there was another distracting set-back. A whole week's worth of work was lost due to one of the most tragic and mysterious incidents to affect the Noatun district since the child-claiming famine of three years before. Two tiny children, a bother and sister both under five years of age, went missing, vanished completely, and in the end were given up for dead. The whole population of the district, Fullay and her helpers included, gave up their days to help in the search for them. This little brother and sister were known as Beel and Hukii Orrurar. They were beautiful children, and unusual in the Noatun district with their corn-yellow hair, skin the colour of golden sand, and both with deep set eyes that shone as blue as summer skies.

The mother of Beel and Hukii was known as Gerda Orrurar. Gerda Wild-eyes. She had worked in the big house of a wealthy mining manager, a powerful, important man from the mine company's headquarters in the city. He was a foreigner, skin like snow, and used to living in ease and luxury.

Gerda had worked as his cook and cleaner. She was a beautiful woman to look upon, and was gentle natured at that time. The manager had fallen in love with her, and she with him, and their love had been passionate, with three children blossoming out of it. But there the fairytale ends. When the company decided to close down its mines in Noatun the manager returned to his life, and real wife, back in his own country. He left his house and lands to the distraught Gerda and her children. With two other children from a widowed marriage, her life had been a struggle, living with the pain of desertion while trying to keep the six of them healthy and fed. Her land was on the very edge of the district, and she rarely ventured into the village. There she was seen as a disgraced outcast, an eccentric who had betrayed her own people by living out of marriage with an official of the mine, and a foreign one at that.

When Beel and Hukii disappeared, poor Gerda lost her sense of reality, madness making her bitter and frenzied, and it was many months before she could even act as a mother again.

The two children vanished one evening while out playing in the scrubland behind their house. Two days later Gerda came wailing and screaming into Noatun, her three other children trailing forlornly behind her. In a ranting frenzy she ran from shack to shack, pounding her fists upon doors, demanding the return of her beautiful children. She blamed the whole village, accusing all who came to listen of stealing away Beel and Hukii

'Haven't you always loathed me?' she shrieked, eyes flashing upon the bewildered crowd that had gathered around her.

'Give them back to me. I know you all whisper against me and hate me for bearing the children of an outsider. But to do this. Aren't you all ashamed?'

Nobody was sure how to handle this sudden, shrieking apparition of madness, and it was Fullay who eventually pushed through the crowd to calm Gerda enough to tell her story.

'They've gone,' she groaned to them, head in her hands. 'The two little ones. My Beel, my Hukii. They were out playing. I saw them, I was watching them a while from my own back window. And I was busy with bread. And then they were gone. They were not back by meal time, and we searched the fields until it was too dark to even see. We called them and called them but.....we've searched everywhere now. Day and night. Not a sign though. Not a footprint. Please, give me back my children! That's all I'm asking....'

She broke down into sobs and wailing while the troubled villagers muttered anxiously between themselves. A search was quickly organised, and all work on the lake ceased, Fullay and her helpers going with the rest of the village to search the district. For a week they searched over the quarries, mine workings and scrub lands of the district. All the poisonous quarry pools were dredged, every field, mineshaft and hillside scoured. But no sign of the children was found, and after ten days of intensive searching the organised search began to fizzle out. All but Gerda had really given up hope for the children, and most feared the worst. Dead, they whispered. Fallen down some impenetrable mineshaft or crushed beneath boulders in a quarry near their home. Kidnapped, others thought. Thieving nomads must have spotted them from the road and lured them away; golden skinned children like Gerda's would fetch a good price in any slave market. Undoubtedly they had been taken to Abasu, the nearest seaport, and were now aboard some slave ship heading west across the ocean.

As others gave up the search, poor Gerda became more frenzied, scratching at the earth for clues and footprints, trying to move huge rocks by herself in the fear that her children were imprisoned beneath them. She went without food or sleep, searched by day and by night, croaking out their names, weeping and ranting and cursing at the sky. When she collapsed through exhaustion, her fingers and feet bleeding from her desperate search, women took the demented Gerda home to comfort and look after her and the other three children. The search for Beel and Hukii came to a halt.

For many years after, people speculated about the tragic fate of those two children, for no bodies were ever found, and not a whisper of them was ever heard from the city.

Only one single person in the Noatun district did know the true fate of Beel and Hukii. Fullay Laharah. Fullay The Lake Builder. Imprisoner of children.

But she had her reasons.

A sun and a moon for thirteen stars.

That was reason enough for her.

Her abduction of the children had pained Fullay to the core of her heart. As a mother, she knew how it was to miss children, to lose them into death, or to their own paths in life. Yet she also understood that all progress and gain in life requires a sacrifice of some form. A loss to a few can be a gain for the many. And so, pushing aside her conscience with this logic, she had walked out to the edges of the district and to Gerda's farmstead, taking great care not to be seen by human eyes. There she hid herself and watched the children of Gerda play on the land around their home. When the moment was right and Fullay knew that she would not be seen by Gerda, she appeared before the two smallest children. With fantastic games, enchanting songs and the promise of specially baked sweetcakes, she lured them on, further and further away from their home. Beneath the shade of a cluster of thorn trees they rested, and she fed them the cakes and water. Drugged cakes, made with a secret blend of sleeping herbs. Before long the children were lost in the depths of a black, peaceful sleep. Fullay sat with them until nightfall, her stomach churning with butterflies as she heard the distant voice of Gerda calling out the names of the lost children. Under the cover of darkness she carried them away like a bundle of firewood upon her back.

    Away by the western edge of the crumbling city road was an old slate quarry, cliff faces pitted with cavern openings. One cavern led into an elaborate network of abandoned mineworkings. The tunnels twisted and turned, black passageways weaving into each other, separating out again like fingers, some branching off to come to sudden endings of solid, impenetrable rock. From her childhood wanderings Fullay knew this labyrinth well. In one dead-end tunnel she remembered a shallow cavity with a narrow neck of an entrance, shaped in the earth like a huge drinking bottle. By the light of a lantern she placed the sleeping children in this cavity, tied their hands and feet together, then gagged their mouths so that they could not shout or scream. There, in utter darkness, she hid her sun and moon, carefully covering the cavity entrance with a slab of shale, leaving just a crack of opening for air. Every other night Fullay returned secretly to her makeshift dungeon. There she untied the children, removed their gags, and gave them food and water. By the flickering light of Fullay's lantern they ate and drank in a trembling, silent terror, too young to even begin to understand what was happening to them. Though she was gentle she never smiled at them, or spoke kind words. She knew that to befriend them would lead to attachment, and that would have made the burden of her guilt even heavier. After they had eaten she would retie and gag them, place the slab back to conceal the cavity entrance, then return home to sleep a little before resuming her work upon the lake.

In the month after the disappearance of Beel and Hukii, work upon the lake and its trenches was all but completed. Nine full phases of the moon had swollen through the sky since Fullay had first struck the earth with her pick-axe. By the light of the tenth full moon, the whole population of Noatun gathered near the spring at the source of their stream. Only a flat hand's width of earth separated the waters of the spring from the feeding trench, and this earth Fullay herself removed with a few swinging strokes of her pick. Like a cascade of jewels, water poured down into the trench, shimmering silver and blue in the moonlight, streaming down hill, a froth of dust and pebbles rolling along at the head of the stream's new path. The crowd whooped and cheered, chasing the stream, dancing and chanting out songs of celebration. All night people danced and sang around the edges of the quarry that was to become their lake. Fullay herself sat brooding in a dark silence, Tyre by her side, both watching dream become reality as a slow stain of moon-glinting water seeped across the shadowed floor of the quarry. By dawn the whole surface was covered with water. Most people of the district took a holiday from any work and settled along the quarry edges to watch the water creep higher and slowly higher up the stone walls. For three days Fullay and Tyre sat upon the lower rim, watching the progress of the water, and though many people came over to congratulate her and to sing her praises, not once did they see her smile or look happy at the progress of her lake. The only time that her stern face relaxed to betray just a flicker of gladness was when water lapped at the lower rim of the quarry and began to pour along the draining trench, flowing back toward the original course of the stream. At that fantastic sight the people of Noatun sang and danced another celebration. Fullay and Tyre hauled themselves to their feet, and when it was quiet enough to be heard Fullay at last spoke to the crowd.

'There, then,' her voice cracked out. 'There's your lake. And forever may it be there. But now the time's come to do something about the fish.'

A worried murmur rippled through the villagers. They were expecting her to request money as contribution toward the cost of fish sprats, but most had little, or nothing, to offer.

'Don't worry, I know your mean hearts,' she scorned. 'I don't want your money. But I do need to make a long journey, and all I ask of you are these simple things. First, I need to borrow two camels. Two strong, healthy ones that won't die or go lame on the road. Then I need two large, strong urns. Clay ones, the kind for storing drinking water. Old, reliable ones that won't crack or leak on the way. Big enough to hold a pig, but not so big that a single camel can't carry them both when filled with water.

And I'll be needing a little food and goodwill from each of you. That's all. Give me these things and you'll see your lake filled with fish soon enough, as sure as I'm standing here.'

She turned from the crowd then, limping with Tyre up hill toward their home, ready to prepare herself for a journey of many days.

By the next morning Fullay had her camels, her two urns, and a supply of food that would well see her through her travels. After saying farewells to Tyre and a few neighbours she set off on her mysterious journey, leaving her destination a secret to all but her husband. That first morning she headed south along the track that led to the old city road, out past the farmstead of Gerdra and her children, and so to the quarry where she had entombed Beel and Hukii. There she camped, and at the first glimpse of dawn she went into the labyrinth to collect the children.

For three weeks she had kept them in that cell of blackness. They had lost all sense of time, of day or night, and were so confused that when Fullay came to untie them and told them that they were to be taken on a great journey, they neither asked her questions nor tried to run away. They were led through the labyrinth of tunnels and out into the first light of dawn. They had grown accustomed to darkness, and they blinked with painful eyes even in the half-light of daybreak as they devoured the breakfast that Fullay set before them. When they had finished eating she loosely tied their hands and wrists again, had the camel with the large urns crouch before her, and into each urn she placed a child. They fitted easily into the urns, and the camel thought little of their weight. The urn lids were covered with sackcloth, tied secure, and then Fullay, her camels and her strange cargo, headed south along the city road, and so out of Noatun.

Six full days they travelled. The journey passed without incident, and on the seventh morning they came to the great, sprawling seaport of Abasu, a teeming, stinking place filled with people from every corner of the world. Ancient motor vehicles, mules and camels with great packs jammed the narrow streets, crowds jostling and bartering at every street junction and in the many markets, wild-eyed sea-men of all races drinking themselves to lewd madness in the countless taverns and hovel-bars.

Hidden away in their urns, the two children trembled with terror, for they had never heard such noise, or smelled such foul and exotic scents. Fullay herself had only ever been to the great port twice in her life, once as a child with her father, and once again with Tyre shortly after their wedding ceremony. The memory of one particular market place had embedded itself in her mind; a place that to her had been a source of horror and fascination. This market lay upon the old quay, out beyond the main trading district and past rows of cargo boats that had been hauled up onto the beach for repair. In this market the merchandise was people - adults and children and even tiny babies. The slave market. As a child, clutching in dread at her father's hand, she had watched as girls and boys of her own age were made to stand on wooden cargo crates and then auctioned off to bearded, sly-eyed traders. Children sold by desperate parents who could no longer feed them and wanted a chance of a good home for them in the west, or auctioned off by traders who had acquired them in place of unpaid debts. Toward this market, through the filthiest and most dangerous districts of the city, Fullay led her camels. Being strong willed and not afraid of the vilest of men, she had scoured the bars around the slave market, listening here, asking questions there, until she found a trader from whom she knew she might get her asking price for her golden skinned children. In a squalid, rat-ridden yard in the fisherman's shanty town, she made Beel and Hukii climb from their urns, then began to bargain hard with the slave-trader. From a gleam in his eyes Fullay knew that he was delighted with the appearances of the children. With their golden hair and skin, their startling blue eyes, there was no doubt that anywhere in the world they would be seen as beautiful. In the west such children would be worth their weight in gold. He bargained bitterly, tried to force her price down, became furious and even stamped out of the yard when she refused to lower her price. As she knew he would, the trader returned within minutes, muttering and shaking his head as he reached into the folds of his cloak, complaining that Fullay's high prices would be the ruin of him and the whole slave-trade. But he paid her price and the bewildered children were handed over to him. Six spheres of silver for Beel, seven spheres of gold for Hukii - this was the price Fullay had demanded so adamantly. Thirteen stars for a sun and a moon. These spheres she hid away in her robes as she watched the children being led away toward the market and the auction boxes. They looked so sad and pathetic, calling out a confusion of goodbyes to Fullay, but her eyes and throat were blocked with tears, and she watched them vanish without a farewell or single word of explanation.

Unable to bear watching the auction of the two, she led her camels with the water urns back to the city and left the port that same afternoon, heading north west up the coast toward the famous fishing town of Medina.

Three days it took her to reach Medina, and here her trading continued. Medina was, and still is, a place of fish markets. A town on the mouth of two rivers where fish, both live and dead, fresh water and salt water, and from all nations of the world, are traded. Some markets were stacked with rows of glass tanks in which exotic, multi-coloured fish flashed and flittered amongst weeds and bubbling water. Some shone like fantastic mini-rainbows, others glowed brightly like lanterns, and Fullay wandered around the markets in amazement at the beauty of the creatures. She saw creatures from the depths of the ocean that she could not have imagined possible in this world, some beautiful, some hideous, and she wondered about the truth of the old Noatun proverb that in Medina it is possible to buy yourself a mermaid. She spoke a great deal to the stall holders and live-fish traders, describing to them in detail the terrain of her home village, the size and the depth of the lake there, and even the quality of the water. After days of talking with experts and traders she used some of her spheres of gold and silver to buy fertilised fish eggs and tiny living sprats of fish that she was assured would survive in the waters of her artificial lake. With more of the money she bought nets and the twine and tools to make them, hooks and lines, and a large supply of dried fish that had her camel straining at the knees with its load. The eggs and sprats she placed in the urns which were filled with fresh water, and the urns she loaded upon the second, stronger camel. The urns were teeming with tiny, glittering lives and were a beautiful sight to peer into, yet Fullay knew that many, or even all of those lives might fade away on the long trek back to Noatun. With trepidation and ill-forboding, she set off through a dust-storm on the long trek home.

Her journey was full of desert storms, of rock-baking days and freezing nights. It took many days longer than she had anticipated, and drained the vitality from Fullay's body and spirit. Twice a day, at morning and at sunset, she took the sackcloth from the urn tops and checked anxiously upon the life within. And each day the teeming glitter faded, a scum of tiny fish corpses floating to the tops of the urns. These Fullay scooped out to scatter on the dusty road, and even though she topped up the urns every day with fresh water, the waters within her urns became black and brackish, and began to stink of death.

By the time she reached Noatun Fullay was walking as if asleep, half dead with exhaustion, her eyes hooded and full of pain. She was dreading the idea that all life within the two urns had perished on the arduous journey; that the two golden children had been taken away and sold for nothing. Many people of the village gathered at the lake's edge as Fullay and her camels came shimmering toward them like some mirage through the desert haze. They had turned out to cheer and celebrate, but so sombre was her mood as she approached that they remained silent, grim faced, and the morbid atmosphere around the lake was more like that of a funeral after a tragic death than a celebration of hope and new life.

Fullay drifted through the crowd in a glaze-eyed, tight mouthed silence, pain and exhaustion etched deeply in the lines upon her face. She did not say a single word until the camels had reached the rim of the lake. There she ordered the camel bearing the urns to kneel and asked people at hand to help her remove them from the camel's harness. In turn the contents of the urns were tipped carefully into the lake. It is said that a heavy, ominous hush crushed down upon the people of Noatun, for as they watched it seemed that nothing but foul smelling, black water came pouring out of the two urns, as though they were pouring death itself into the fresh waters. But then cries of excitement burst out and Fullay flung herself to her knees in thankfulness. From the brackish stain of the urn waters, like flashes of lightning from a black cloud, flitted glittering, tiny fish. Thirteen fish in all, it is said; seven as bright as golden sunshine, six pale silver, the colour of the midnight moon.

A small start, but even by the next year over a hundred healthy fish were counted in the waters of Fullay's lake. The year after, five hundred, and after that too many to even count. They thrived and grew in their thousands, and when nets were cast into the waters there were enough fish in a single catch to feed the whole village for weeks. The terraces around the lake side flourished and were shady with the canopies of young trees. Birds nested in the tree branches and children played in the green shade. By the day of Fullay's death, five years after the completion of her lake, crops and fruits were being harvested from the terraced gardens there.

The people in Noatun these days are a healthy lot when compared to the hungry of the world. No children there go hungry now, and death due to malnutrition is unheard of throughout the region. Fullay the Lake Builder is remembered as a saint and saviour, as a person who transformed an insane dream into a practical and beautiful reality.

Yet it is still recounted that from the day her lake was completed until the hour of her death, not even a flicker of a smile crossed her grim and weathered face. Hence her name, Fullay The Grim.

A woman whose heart, so it is said, ached for the suffering of the children in this world.

Chris Firth

If you've enjoyed this and previous stories by Chris Firth in *Dream Catcher* you've been in the ELECTRAGLADE

E
L
E
C
T
R
A

G
L
A
D
E

ELECTRAGLADE is an award winning collection of inter-linked short stories by Chris Firth, published together for the first time by SINAP Press available from SNNAP direct via www.skrev-press.com or via amazon £6.99
ISBN 1-904646-00-X

Masterful Storytelling - twenty first century fiction at its best.

The Sheathed Smile

Serious discussions always took place
in the hall, a corridor between the kitchen
and the party wall the family shared
with the pub next door.

There was a telephone
on a small polished table,
a vase of flowers and on the wall
a pitted oval mirror,
a shillelagh and hara-kiri sword
whose blade he'd unsheath now and then
just to feel his nerve ends curl.

An airlock between domestic pressure
and the dizzy atmospherics of the street,
it's where household wisdom was dispensed;
where his father failed the facts of life,
the stern mask slipping with relief
to be told: 'Oh, I know all about that';
where the rules they played by were explained:
'We don't expect much of you, but knowing
right from wrong's what matters most.
And whatever you do,
don't make an exhibition of yourself.'

While these words seeded in his brain
the sword's smile carried him amok
into imagined futures
where fame or notoriety
embraced him like a samurai.

Mike Barlow

REPORT

A woman in a cream silk sari edged with gold
was pushing a buggy along the crowded broadway,
frowning thoughtfully, glancing into the shops.
A little boy trailed after her.
I followed, invisible.
She smoothed back her long dark hair,
blown about in the noisy sunshine,
then spotted something, turned
and disappeared into a shop,

but he didn't realise, toddling along,
dodging adults and oncoming pushchairs,
his black head submerged in the waves
of big pale people approaching the crossing.
'Oh God,' I thought, and he stopped, suddenly struck
with panic, began crying 'Mammy, mammy!'
turning desperately this way and that,
but no-one saw or heard
or thought it their business.

I could still see
her calm beautiful face,
bent over the goods. A man
noticed the child, and hesitated.
Then I was there,
brushed the boy's shoulder,
whispered 'this way' inaudible
above the roar of traffic,
and led him back to the shop,

The Sheathed Smile

Serious discussions always took place
in the hall, a corridor between the kitchen
and the party wall the family shared
with the pub next door.

There was a telephone
on a small polished table,
a vase of flowers and on the wall
a pitted oval mirror,
a shillelagh and hara-kiri sword
whose blade he'd unsheath now and then
just to feel his nerve ends curl.

An airlock between domestic pressure
and the dizzy atmospherics of the street,
it's where household wisdom was dispensed;
where his father failed the facts of life,
the stern mask slipping with relief
to be told: 'Oh, I know all about that';
where the rules they played by were explained:
'We don't expect much of you, but knowing
right from wrong's what matters most.
And whatever you do,
don't make an exhibition of yourself.'

While these words seeded in his brain
the sword's smile carried him amok
into imagined futures
where fame or notoriety
embraced him like a samurai.

Mike Barlow

REPORT

A woman in a cream silk sari edged with gold
was pushing a buggy along the crowded broadway,
frowning thoughtfully, glancing into the shops.
A little boy trailed after her.
I followed, invisible.
She smoothed back her long dark hair,
blown about in the noisy sunshine,
then spotted something, turned
and disappeared into a shop,

but he didn't realise, toddling along,
dodging adults and oncoming pushchairs,
his black head submerged in the waves
of big pale people approaching the crossing.
'Oh God,' I thought, and he stopped, suddenly struck
with panic, began crying 'Mammy, mammy!'
turning desperately this way and that,
but no-one saw or heard
or thought it their business.

I could still see
her calm beautiful face,
bent over the goods. A man
noticed the child, and hesitated.
Then I was there,
brushed the boy's shoulder,
whispered 'this way' inaudible
above the roar of traffic,
and led him back to the shop,

where at last she was running out,
looking up and down the street,
her mouth a gasp of anxiety.
'There,' I said, unheard, pushing him
into her arms. Her brown eyes
met my see-through ones,
and she seemed to murmur 'thank you'
to thin air. Was that all?
I thought so and came home.

Angela Rigby

SEPARATION

In the hotel room
I open
my two large
suitcases
and see
how carefully
you packed them
for me this morning.

I am afraid
to unpack —
the distance
between us
will suddenly
be real.

Ian Seed

CORPSE

You lie in your coffin
in the front room of the house
that you shared with your third
wife and family.

Your eldest son, I move as
a guest through the small crowd
of half-brothers and sisters.
Later I sneak in the dark

to look at you alone. Light
flickers in from the street
and across your face wavers
a smile of welcome.

Ian Seed

**DAD —
NOT DEAD**

When the Americans
unnecessarily dropped an atom bomb on Nagasaki
they sort of dropped it on my dad.

He was miles below
the blast, miles below the town.
Below. Below — down a mine. A slave, POW.

Without clothes.
Shovelling coal in the dust by the light of a candle.

Stephen Baker

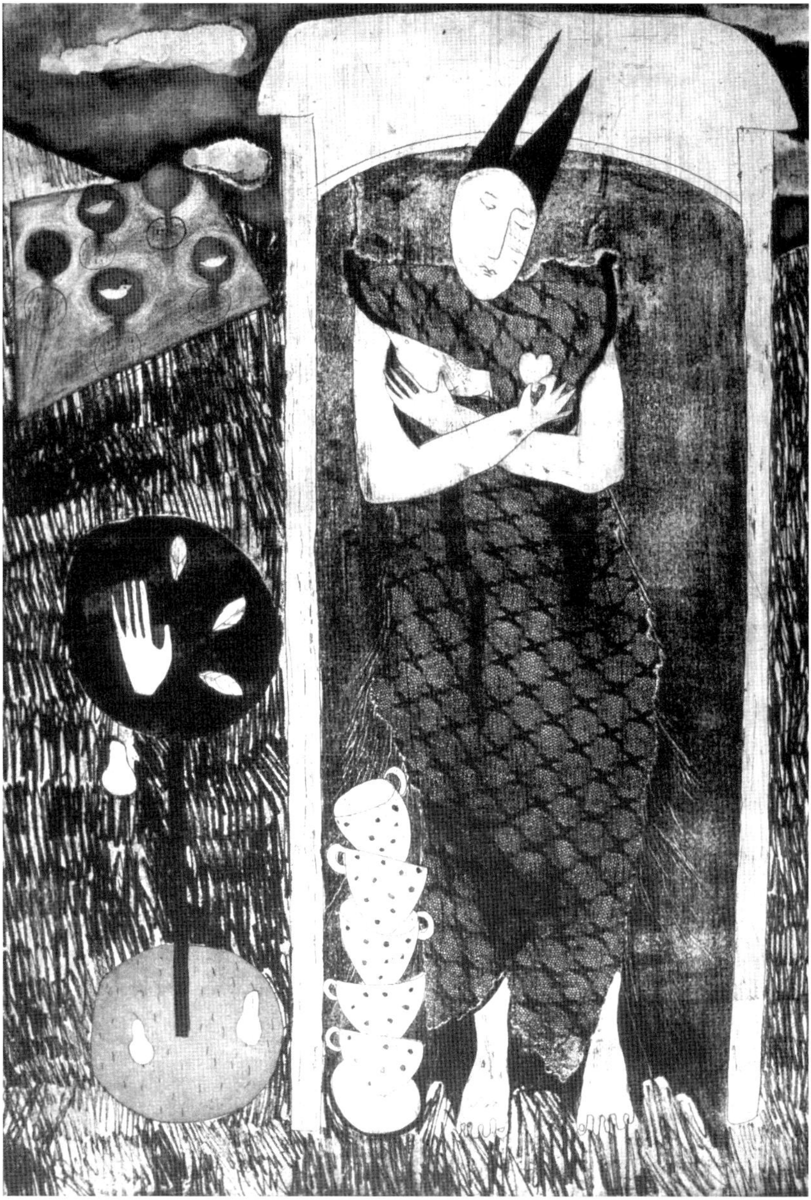

DEAR FATHER My father drowned himself last year.
Drove into the local river.

His coupé squelched him in.

The night before his death,
he laid
his lanky body next to my mother's
like a map, his West
Coast against her East Coast.

She laced his neck with her
lemon-fingers,
sugaring his heart, curling
his mysterious holes.

He found no truth in her lakes.

When they jerked him up, he
was 15 degrees below
freezing, a clump of lucid glass.

I kept his letters — a series
of fractured
plumes — his own plumes,
his wife's and mine.

It appeared he had attempted
this before, but
failed, seduced and
lost in a
rumbling storm of pain:

My mother's cyclones, tearing up his highlands.

She remarried soon enough —
my uncle — a fat man who had
gone through a previous family.

Juned Subhan

WATER

What was it
made you end your life —
some experience in your missionary work,
the depression
which haunted your schooldays?

And as you walked
deep into that cold water
did you recall those dark afternoons
in the music room,
at the piano beside Mr Cullen,
trying to master
Chopin's Raindrop Prelude.

I remember you then
pale faced, golden haired,
incapable of violence,
until now.

Joseph Allen

Roads

Often we find roads
that seem to go nowhere

mirages on winter afternoons
precarious boundaries across rough bog-land

or climbing between bare hills
veined with dry-stone walls

to a sky's opening.

And where are the farmhouses?
as if stone returns to stone

and all we are left with
is squares of birch.

Yet there is more than work left undone
or abandoned with disuse,
simply forgotten

there is a moment of recognition
when we find ourselves alone and unprotected,

like lying with your face close to the earth
and the quickness of a blow

that shuts out the watery light.

I have a road,
that dips to a copse of pine

where it is dripping cool and dark —
here I found touch and loneliness.

Gary Allen

WATER

What was it
made you end your life —
some experience in your missionary work,
the depression
which haunted your schooldays?

And as you walked
deep into that cold water
did you recall those dark afternoons
in the music room,
at the piano beside Mr Cullen,
trying to master
Chopin's Raindrop Prelude.

I remember you then
pale faced, golden haired,
incapable of violence,
until now.

Joseph Allen

Roads

Often we find roads
that seem to go nowhere

mirages on winter afternoons
precarious boundaries across rough bog-land

or climbing between bare hills
veined with dry-stone walls

to a sky's opening.

And where are the farmhouses?
as if stone returns to stone

and all we are left with
is squares of birch.

Yet there is more than work left undone
or abandoned with disuse,
simply forgotten

there is a moment of recognition
when we find ourselves alone and unprotected,

like lying with your face close to the earth
and the quickness of a blow

that shuts out the watery light.

I have a road,
that dips to a copse of pine

where it is dripping cool and dark —
here I found touch and loneliness.

Gary Allen

A Matter of Time

Day, but still dark.
The rain a reminder
of how many mornings have begun like this.

Here, for longer than is known,
lamps have been lit
where winter roused past villagers for work.

I switch on a bedside light.
5 a.m., and the house still quiet
but for the soft-clawed scratching of cold rain.

It is a comfort
to stretch once more beneath
a blanket that has sheltered me all night.

Brief comfort, maybe,
yet one my neighbours
under the headstones of their churchyard beds

would gladly share,
stretching their limbs towards
first cock-crow breaking through the dark -

the time so short between
those who extend their sleep
and we who wake each morning after snow.

The only difference
this day's light can make
is whether before the Spring our faith will crack.

Edward Storey

THE DEAD

Who are they -
nine-tenths pressed to peat or chalk
stewed bones resisting
that last squeeze into nothing?

A few
extricate themselves - percolate
their stale-sweet plasmin
through grave-roots' sieves to leave

in the trench
their spent throws of cinnamon stick.
The remaining you might
glimpse - if you put your eyes out

of focus -
swimming in that syncopated instant
in-between what is
recognised and what was seen.

So deadly clever
they are. Can hide in a blink
Be wary then how
you raise a knife. Or *schlock* it down.

Sometimes
to make it easy on us they stand - wait
plain as daylight
in our sleep. Or shimmer at the edges

of pylons
as though the gas there had thickened
slightly - a plankton
of faces making of air serous jelly.

Or - close up -
they are as sunlight that for ages spates
between sparse molecules
then at last arrives to impress itself in skin.

Mario Petrucci

Shaping Destiny

The car labours over Saddleworth moor
towards night. Greys and browns;
darker shrub. The eye holds
this no-land of the dead unhappily.
A place to pass through; leave behind.

Twisting in her seat, breath sharp
with five-year-old wonder — *The World!*
Craters of a moon landscape,
lumps of desert rock,
a planet uninhabited,
desolate with its own emptiness.

I smile, securely belted.
The World is round.
And from the square box of my mind
pull spheres and galaxies;
a space-rocket;
teach her infinitesimal and universal;
mark our place.

The car climbs, juddering.
I'm on top of the world!
she yells, defiant, to the night,
digging straight to its centre,
proving them wrong.

    And suddenly
I see it too, pock-marked
and spreading, spreading like the sea,
the horizon its edge.
Stars are winking above,
close enough to reach on wings.

Look! I could stretch one arm skyward,
my fingers prick in turn
each beautiful,
perfectly obvious point.

Cathy Grindrod

On the Theft of a 4,000 Year Old Fish from a Village Museum in Scotland

We make our own truths.

It was a child. She took it in a shopping bag,
like weekend bread, instinctive, necessary,

made her steady way down cliff paths
edged with thrift. Small pebbles parted,
made her going easy.

A hush about the waves,
a perfect tide — unforecast.
A village shut its doors.

The oyster-catcher, watching,
did not call. Cliffs closed ranks.
Kneeling in their shelter, easing it from dark,
she cradled it within the light of early dusk,

walked toward the water's edge —
shingle, shells, humped strings of swollen bladderwort.

Beside the line of separation,
a clear beyond. Bending low,
she whispered into cloth,
reached out with both small arms.

A single gull patrolled the headland,
eyes picking out the tiny form below.

A sudden breeze across the sea; a seagull's cry;
a child who ever after kept her silence;

let things lie.

Cathy Grindrod

SILVER HEART

I'd say it was coincidence:
except we found it after our first night,
washed up among dead starfish

on the beach — something the tide
had rolled around, heaved up
and finished with. The salt

had taken off its shine. At dawn
the sea and sky and shore
were stretched out in a long blurred line

that had no clear beginning
and no end. And there it was
half-hidden in the sand,

no bigger than your smallest fingernail;
inviting us to put it down to fate —
a gift extracted from the turning sea.

'Not fate' I whispered as we kissed
and it disclosed its ever-changing light.
'Not fate but synchronicity.'

Ian Parks

DUNE SHOW   Hear the whispered symphony
of spartina and marram
and watch the little skipper flap
and flutter through ladies' bedstraw.
See the holly-blue flicker from ragwort to yarrow
in pollen mist blown by an estuary sneeze

Through dune curtains observe
the gentle drama of a river mirage
where long-boats and ferries drift
on contradictory currents;
whalers and trawlers fade
down the road between the banks;
and tankers and tugs slip by the shifting spit

Rest on this mare's tail cord-grass bed
decked in red and white clover
and bird's foot trefoil.
Watch sand and weed embrace
spring-tide debris and the litter of men.

Behind the buckthorn veil
let the rattling, panting train pass
and distant accents soften
to echoes of grasshopper and bee.

Gordon Wilson

A New Eden

I dream of a place where man does not exist
Where trees grow tall and strong and are as kings
Where gentle waters wash the lovely land
And bright fish swim in aqueous splendour.

Here the lion roars for joy and all the natural world
Exults in its own kingdom.
Golden Apollo once again is seen on his diurnal throne
And glowing gods and nymphs, shy fairies and quick elves
Return and mingle with the glorious creatures
Bringing them food and drink and
Playing music to them on strange pipes and lutes
Charming the wind and waves into a wondrous chorus
Which soars to Mount Olympus

Where satisfied Zeus, in his eternal court, smiles
Remembering that extinct and violent aberration, man,
Then smiles again, blessing all that lives
In this now peaceful Eden.

India Russell

The Dinner Party

Last night, I had a dinner party
With Wilfred Owen, Harold Monro
And Borges.

We drank wine, laughed, forgot to eat
And of course, wept freely.
I told them how I loved their work
How long-ago I used to recite, 'The wind feels cold enough
Tonight to crack the stars and bring them down'
On my way to my Saturday morning speech and drama class,
Learning it as I walked; how Owen's, 'Move him into the sun'
Had always moved me and how the truthfulness
Of Borges gave me hope in this untruthful time.

We stayed up late, musing and reading, reciting
And drinking and finally it was I who was tired -
They were ready to go on till morning and beyond -
But I was heady and drowsy with their terrible beauty
And then, as we parted, they said, 'And
You too are one of us. We know. We understand.'

India Russell

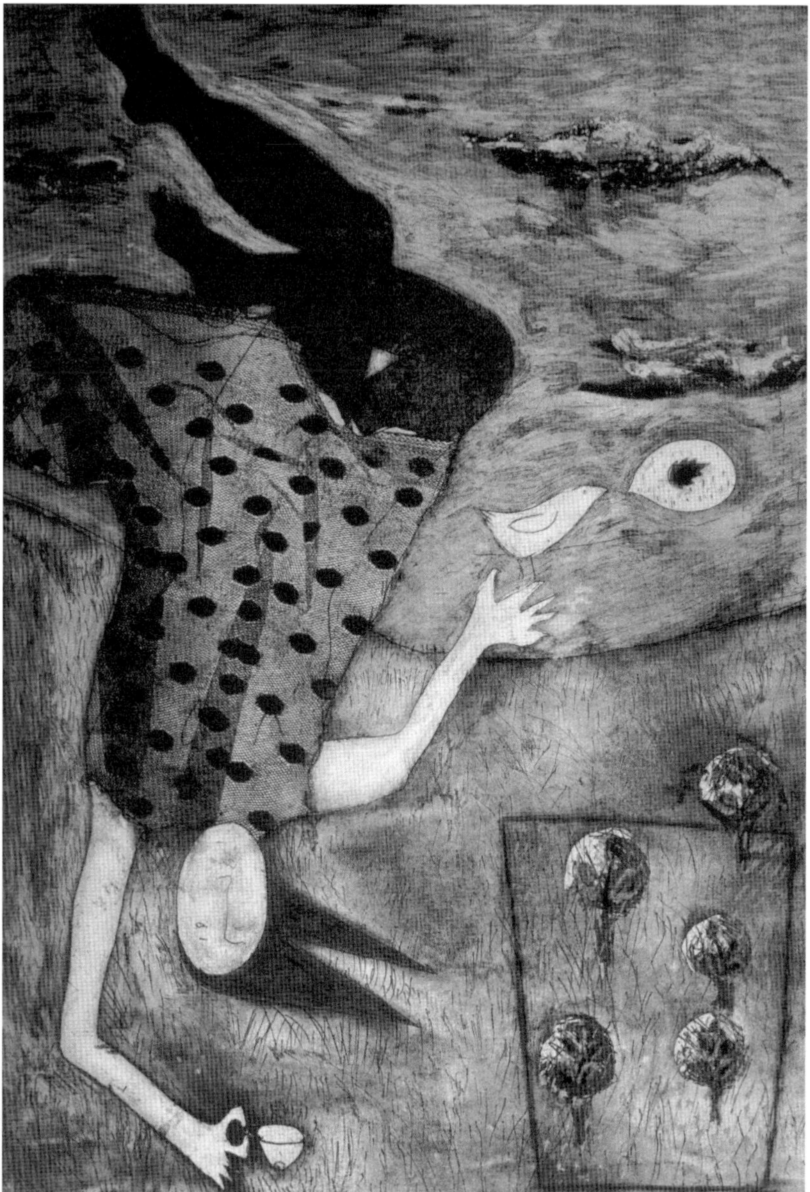

THE LOST CHILD

I had run out of ground coffee, the brand my husband likes. Blue Mountain. I don't know whether it is the name or the taste he likes most. 'Blue Mountain,' he says, rolling the words with his lips. A far away look in his eyes. An expression I never see when he looks at me. Normally I keep a reserve in but the children had just gone back to school after chickenpox and I was totally disorganized.

Feeling like a breath of fresh air, I decided to walk to the shops instead of taking the car. It was a fresh fine morning in late October. Fine weather for Hallowe'en. Not that I was letting my children out tonight. Not after just going back to school. I wasn't keen on Hallowe'en anyway. All those old people being terrified out of their wits by dressed up children!

The shops were only ten minutes' walk away and I knew I was sure to meet a friend or two to chat to.

Before I could buy the coffee, I saw that outside the chemist a small crowd had gathered. I wormed my way to the front. There was a young woman, whom I didn't at first recognise, crying to distraction. What struck me most forcibly was not so much her distress as the fact that she seemed more dressed for the catwalk than for a visit to the shops. Except that she had no make up on, which was why I didn't recognise her.

I took in her straight tight purple coat-dress, an intense reddish purple like ripe plums. It was gathered to one side over her large breasts with a brooch, swaying earrings, hair piled on top, skinny hips and long thin legs ending in preposterously high heeled sandals.

Then I realised who she was, she had moved in a few doors down about two years ago. I knew her only to smile at. She was always very smartly dressed, even in casual wear. A neighbour told me the newcomer was a model. She had made herself notorious by claiming to have been attacked in her garden by an intruder while she was sunbathing. The intruder had never been caught. And several people had dismissed it as fantasy. I didn't know what to believe and kept an open mind. I was away with my husband and family on an exchange in Canada at the time so the furore had died down by the time we had come home. But soon after the incident she had become pregnant.

She had had the baby a couple of months previously. But the little girl was reported to be sickly.

The young woman waved a parcel, tears running down her face.

'My baby! I want my baby.'

I asked the woman next to me what had happened and she explained that Olivia, for that was the young woman's name - I knew it could be nothing common like Jane or Anne - it had to be Olivia - had gone into the chemist to buy a toy for her baby, leaving her outside and when she came back, the baby had gone.

By this time, the police had arrived in the shape of a young policewoman who looked built for action. Unlike Olivia who was purely ornamental. I found myself volunteering to go home with Olivia. I was a staff nurse on a children's ward so I knew how to deal with people in shock. Also I had a day off.

We went home in a police car with the policewoman.

We went into her house, it was, as I would have expected, up to the minute, glossy wallpaper, thick beige carpets. But there was an over pervading smell of sick, of sourness.

'My baby's always sick,' sobbed Olivia, 'She needs plenty to drink. It's time for her next bottle.'

'Has she got jaundice?' I asked.

Olivia nodded and started to sob again.

I didn't like the sitting room. The only signs of a child in the house was a box of toys in a corner by the door. There was a collection of masks on one wall. African tribal masks, carnival masks. One in particular made me shudder. It was coffee brown with curving yellow stripes on the cheeks like bones. Out of each cheek sprang a sharpened tusk. This mask fixed my eyes for a few seconds until I was able to break the spell.

On another wall was a display of Olivia's modelling photos. She would never make an actress, I thought, she had so few expressions. And below them there were photos of the baby, a pretty looking child though with a definite sun tan, symptomatic of jaundice. The shape of the face and the eyes reminded me of my youngest daughter who had been an exceptionally pretty baby.

There was a bookcase of glossy books mostly on witchcraft and some on travel.

The policewoman invited Olivia to sit down and then started to ask questions. There was a background of phone and doorbell ringing, which went on more or less all day. Journalists, neighbours, casual passers by. Olivia's parents were abroad and she didn't know where her husband was. He travelled a lot with his job. When the questions had finished, I said, 'Go and lie down.' I helped her upstairs and out of those unlikely clothes.

The bedroom was very tidy, no make up or clothes lying about. On a white settee by the window was ranged a collection of furry animals. Their glassy eyes were fixed and staring. They had something in common with hers.

I went down to the policewoman.

'I can stay with her for a bit,' I said.

The policewoman left.

I went into the kitchen and there saw the washing machine full of baby clothes. For something to do, I hung them up on a rack.

I assembled a tray of tea, with enough for two, and a couple of cheese sandwiches. I was feeling dry and hungry. I poured myself a cup. I would make myself a sandwich later.

Everything in the larder was very neat. Alongside the selection of teas, quite varied, which made me think better of Olivia, was an untouched packet of Blue Mountain. But I left it where it was and reached for the nearest tea which was Kee Mun. There was a white mug with a pink love knot and Olivia in gold above it in the front of the china cupboard but I ignored it for a plain blue one. I took the tray upstairs.

Olivia was lying in bed, uttering moans as if in physical pain, her eyes focussed on the ceiling.

I left her. A door into another room was open and I went in out of curiosity. There was a computer. I agitated the mouse and got E mail. And there was a message. 'Can't stand life with you anymore, all your crying and dramatics. I'm moving out. Chris.'

The doctor arrived, our doctor, very chatty and sympathetic, and prescribed sedation. He enquired after the children. I knocked up a neighbour who agreed to collect the prescription.

The house, the situation was beginning to get me down. Those masks, the absent husband.

I rang up my next door neighbour who had a girl the same age as my eldest daughter and she agreed to collect the children from school. And there was no coffee for my husband. He wouldn't be pleased.

I went out into the garden to get a breather. All around me was the fence the husband had put up soon after the alleged attack. Just inside it were tall bushy shrubs. The house was like a fortress. A tiny apple dropped down with a thud, making me start.

And then I heard a noise, a little cry, a whimper. It came from beyond the fence, in the fence was set a gate. I went to the gate and found myself in a copse. There, under a tree, half covered with leaves and grass was a tiny parcel.

I went up to it. It was a baby. A small cold baby. The lost child.

Then I turned round at a noise. There was Olivia, her face made up, in a dress with daisies on. She was staring straight ahead, her eyes set, in a face of stone, far more terrible than that mask I had seen earlier. She reached out her arms.

Mary Knight

VISUAL BLINDS
of Hollings Road Bradford support new writing!

www.visualblinds.co.uk *for blinds*

www.skrev-press.com *for ground breaking short fiction*

01274 723772 for stress free quote *or free blind advise*

MINIATURES

Sleep
 the peeling of onionskins
layer by layer
to an inner core

    In the shop
    woman bare ankles
    ready to paddle into shoes

        Divorce
        the avalanche of hate
        as he goes ski-ing in Denver

    She's full of
    summer slices
    and love song sounds

    Her blue lace skin
    smells wantingly
    wild

John Greeves

DRAWING CIRCLES

Forgive me if I'm wrong
but I think it was Leonardo
who could draw a perfect circle,

freehand. A useful trick at parties,
one sure to impress the crowd.
Like the man beached at the shoreline
of the room, who sits down

unobserved at the piano and after
a practiced scale or two, trickles into
Embraceable You, flawless as Gershwin.

And before the last tinkling note
falls like a leaf through the silence,
every woman in the room is gathered there,
drawn to him; a perfect circle.

James Caruth

THE PERFORMANCE

Spring pummels the remains
of winter's crust,
scarlet buds
rocket through the soil
and I grey the day
with fact

We did not come here
for God as a witness,
we came here
for the pink spume
of cherry blossom,
the glossalalia of Starlings
in the spire
and the scent
of faith soaked stone.

You try to defy
the new green sap in your veins
and play the red devil
tap dancing and tempting me
from your gravestone stage
as a rusty organ melody
bleeds through
the stained glass body
of Adam.

Gaia Holmes

BILLY MOON

Moon ingrained behind blue mist;
an ink silhouette of buildings.
Jazz streams from a car radio.
People come and go.
Kids monopolise part of the car park
under barley coloured lamps.

A scuffle breaks out.
A Scottish wild cat,
'Get off me you fucking cow!'
three Safeway girls grapple.
Butcher joins in; a shirt
ripped off the back, vodka bombs explode.

Jazz band plays -
another era:
drummer solos, glad to be free
among shoppers. Tight-jeaned lassies,
kids on skate boards, scooters
doing party tricks.

Pensioner complains, claims
he's frightened on the parking lot.
He'll stop shopping here.
'Police are already there,'
check-out girl says.
He goes to have a word.

'He's over-reacting,' says a woman,
'Just kids with nowhere to go.'
Outside the police van stands silent.
A young cop who resembles Paul Scholes
talks to the pensioner, who points
to cheeky kid with a gapped-toothed grin.

Jazz sax blows to Billy Blue Moon
slinking low in the sky. Safeway closes.
The car park is a silent amber glow.
The town, alive with take-a-ways
fish 'n' chips,
Nile Pizza busy.

Liam, drunk with nowhere to go
sits on a corner bench. On the green
roses behind him are luminous white.
Think of Tommy Cooper and laughs:
'Just like that! he says.
The quintet has moved on:

materialised by the mud flats
trumpet player wears a velvet cloak,
white spats, floppy purple hat
stands on a scrubbed white boulder.
A fox watches from the thicket
wondering how he got here.

Piano player in blue satin jacket
starts laying down a boogie beat;
bass and sax melt in.
Trumpet hits a high note,
keeps it there. A young couple dance
as if it happened every night.

Peter Lewin

A God

Just closing the door,
quick, leaving home before dawn,
you smell the street -
damp stones, a tang of metal, the cold,
and the forwardness of the steps and puffs of breath,
the velvet darkness on the move, the starkness
of early things down on the pavement,
sparse coughs lighting it like sparks;
instants of a god in a rush, on the threshold,
whispering with no words but elation,
a nimble sky that touches and goes,
the sprightly wave of a sidelong glance
between hurry and silence.

Davide Trame

Five Notes on the Trumpet

I suppose you might expect to hear
about jazz clubs and how cool it all was,
about Bird and Miles and all of that,
and again how cool it was, yeah man, so cool.

I could talk about classical music
and describe the sweet high sound that soars
above everything in baroque concertos
and that still might not interest you,

but the trumpet is also associated
with gladiatorial shows, and more widely
with ancient wars. I like the idea
that it symbolised power and glory,

but of course the greatest power of all
will use the trumpet to announce the last day,
when all will be judged, and it is of course
the instrument of choice of the angels.

I accept that this seems dated today,
so perhaps I will just tell you the truth
about a poor kid who wanted to play,
and perhaps even more to own, the trumpet.

Stuart Flynn

GIRL, INTERRUPTED AT HER MUSIC

She suddenly sees the silent door open
In the corner of her mind.
A dark bird flies into her memory
And she is lost, alone among others
Distant voices in other rooms.
An echoing pain around her ears,
Fighting her way across the rose petals
Thrown across the shimmering cinder path.

Sitting there she looks out across bridges
Moutains opening up to lies and truth
Hidden among the children on the sand.
She wants to dance to the music of silence
By herself within a moment
A whisper on the wind.
Locked inside Alcatraz
She makes her way home.

Erin L. Hickey

In the Blood

My mother talked to me the other day about my grandfather;
usually, she doesn't care to talk much about the past,
having left it behind her as fast as she could run.
Like a child who broke a vase or tore her dress,
she prefers not to remember things she did.

But in the rusty iron cold of a late autumn day
she said, without warning, in the middle of another conversation,
that I had been her father's favourite.
Did I remember? Did I remember waiting
for him to come home when I was very small,
impatiently standing by the door,
when the afternoon turned slowly to dusk and I knew,
without the knowledge of clocks, it was time.

I would run out to him as soon as he opened the gate;
he would catch me up and swing me into the air,
laughing, then carry me indoors.
Did I remember? Did I remember how he would
pick me up out of bed at night when I woke and was afraid
and sing softly as he walked around the room with me
in his arms; he never did that for her, she said,
when *she* was a baby, and her face closed against memories.

But I don't remember my grandfather.
The journey has been long and hard and I smell winter in the air.
I don't remember - but I have a feeling, physical, unreasonable,
that seems to see the image of him,
melancholy and out of step with the marching world,
dark eyes gazing at horizons whose distances he finally reached
when his congested heart clenched into a savage fist
and ceased to beat; ceased to be the rhythm that
bought me safe back to sleep and quiet dreams.

I don't remember; but my own heart,
sharing his ruined blood, won't forget.

Joolz Denby
(www.joolz.net)

WHAT?

What are you doing?
I'm gloating over his death.
Are you ill?
No, but it feels great.
Why?
Because, because he started
to touch me at nine years old.
Why did he touch you,
Why allow him to?
Didn't you have parents?
He had my parents in his pockets.
Authority oozed from him.
Besides parents were ignorant.
Why? Why? Why?
You wouldn't understand.
How it is.
The power struggle between
the condemned.
Rest now you've been up all
night and you are very tired.
I can't rest. I have to write.
I have to gloat and glow.
Stop it! It's bad for you!
Can't.
At daybreak and sunset,
I feel alive because he is dead.
Time to get up.
Time is all that's left.
And that's ebbing away.

Fatma Durmush

In the Grand Hotel, Lincoln

Sitting, drinking coffee on my own
On the same sofa I've sat on countless times.
This is one of my places; I've been here
With friends of mine, to discuss our poetry,
Our musings and our lives with a caffeine buzz,
And with my girlfriend, before we went away
To Italy, excitement filling our stomachs,
And the coffee we drank whirling us up, light-headed.

Now I sit, dropped, with all these memories.
Nostalgia brings me here to spend my money
In this half-hour, with nothing else to do.
My train will then arrive to take me home,
And my memories discarded here, as with
Soap operas, will be remembered on returning,
Which I will do with friends, my girlfriend, someone.

I've stayed here, often, on my father's visits,
And still do, when he comes, from time to time.
The rooms are at best cosy, at worst cramped,
But I like them; they are my childhood's rooms:
In wonky, strange guesthouses I found the idol
Of my childhood, who brought me evening meals
And took me for daytrips when I saw him, monthly,

For a weekend. I remember hating the time
That I would have to go home. We'd look for the taxi,
And I'd pray it didn't come. It always did.
We'd step outside, and as I'd enter the car
The lump in my throat would expand, to fill my eyes
With silent tears that nobody detected,
As I turned my head to catch his final blown kiss.

Rory Waterman

If Only
(we could trick fate)

If only
That morning
I could've orchestrated a minor tragedy
Perhaps had tripped from the ladder
Hurting my back
Keeping you off work

Or perhaps
A stabbing dart of pain
Had flicked your heart
'Rest a while,'
The doctor could've worryingly whispered

If only
Our four-year-old monster had cast his spell
Climbed over you like his favourite hill
Pulled your tie
Turned your spotless suit into a mess of creases
Clutched your mighty hairy hand in his rebellious grip
And cried, 'Papa I want you to drop me off at school.'

If only I'd held your marching steps
With a lusty smile and a glint in the eye,
That silly expression, our coded word,
You would've known what it meant
If only I'd poured into it
All the world's lust and coyness
Drew you back
Irresistibly to my warm confines.

If only the sun's rays hadn't pierced
So early through our window-panes
The alarm had failed to go off
We'd over-slept
If somehow I'd kept you home
If only that morning we could've tricked fate.

Divya Mathur; translated from Hindi by Salman Asif

TRAPS

When I put my hand
To the cold glass,
There would be a clue,
And it would be winter.
What crime would the law's
Powder and prints show,
Dusting the past?
Seeing my print against
The end of summer,
The end of open doors
And a shortage of heat.
No need now to gut the earth
Of its fossilised past.
If it were guilt,
The evidence as sharp as glass
That brought me down,
I would be a kind man
And die in want.
More cut off from words
Than a seal, and afraid.

Norman Jackson

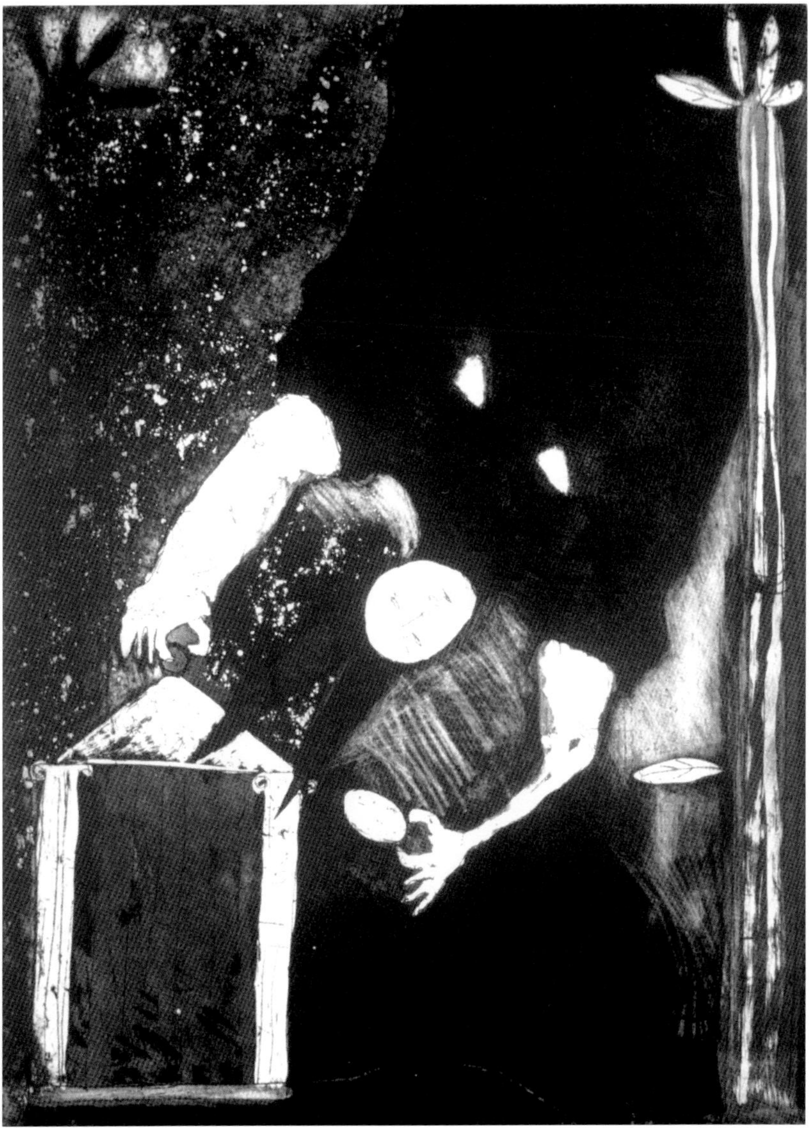

WAKE UP

My self each flake but also the snowfall entire,
I fall toward sleep, taking
shapes from the ground that waits below.
Mutilations. A slow ragged
severing of my testicles
with cold water and blows
hurled into my face to keep me conscious.
First the right, then the left
eyeball sucked from the socket
(my head in a vise)
until each dangles from its strong
optic nerve, then the strings are wrapped
around two fingers and wetly plucked
from my brain.   Forgive me, my love,
for telling you. Forgive me, but
you lie beside me in the dark.
Here in the borderland, disassembled,
accumulating, my body
has fallen into the torturer's hands,
and I can descend no further. Two friends
died last year, conformed themselves
to the waiting ground. Forgive me
if I writhe and kick and hiss breath
into my lungs, and force myself to try
to cross the only other border,
clutching your hand and whispering
Wake up.

J. Morris

LA SAINTE CHAPELLE, PARIS

The upper chapel looks entirely made of glass,
stonework receding to invisible, centuries

ahead of Cartier floating diamonds on thin
gauge platinum like frost, like fur. The cold

starts at my head, creeps down my neck. I wrap
my scarf, but this is stone cold seeping cell by cell

out to my shoulders down my back, aching
for a cloak of heavy skins stitched tight and lined

with velvet, heat of the thousand candles
lit for evening Mass here in St Louis' reliquary.

But I'd be downstairs anyway, climbing
from the servants' chapel, taper trembling,

empty hand smoothing up the metal rail,
lighting one, then two, then three. Hurry, for the

jewelled windows dance and whisper
waiting for the flames to settle, Apostles stern

around the walls, Last Judgement shining
violet, jade and turquoise sins upon my face.

When everything is lit and shadowless,
the stories brighten. Saints and flowers,

miracles and resurrection. Voices spin
the chill air, curl like incense, rise ornate

and indecipherable, hang, then settle over seven
hundred years, to English, German, Japanese,

the swish of laminated information cards
narrating how King Louis won his primacy

among the feudal lords by bringing home
the crown of thorns, a splinter of the cross.

I bring this postcard home. Fourth window
on the south side, Judith, lilac, pale and naked,

bathing in a fountain with a bar of blackberry
scented, muted purple soap from La Samaritaine.

Nell Farrell

FOUR COURSES

I am doing the washing.
I am cooking dinner for three.
I am setting words on a screen.

My dead grandmother would be incredulous.
My dead mother would be unimpressed.
My daughter takes it for granted.

Pamela Lewis

A GOD JUST UNDER THE GROUND

These Mexicans
bow down their heads as they walk along the railroad tracks in
downtown L.A.
toward this factory
because they know
there is a god just under the ground that can toss them
like matchsticks
They peddle
little bikes with high handlebars to work
and look
at the sky as breathe in the air
from the sea and the mountains and hold it
in their hearts as their hands throw the handles
to the machines
and bow down their heads
because a music
in the stars comes out of their radios in the guitars
of their songs
and there is beauty
in those stars and songs no one
will ever explain they bow
down their heads because they will never really want to rule
the earth because
the blood on the sidewalk from a gang bullet
could be theirs and if anyone
ever has to hang from a cross like Jesus it could be
their brother
in jail they bow
down their heads because their women are so beautiful
and L.A. river once flowed
a block away and will again
some day when all our concrete and steel has crumbled
into dust these Mexicans
place their radios on the workbenches beside their machines

and listen to the music of the mariachis
and gaze at the beautiful long hair of their women
and bow down their heads
because they are so grateful
the blood
flows in their veins.

Fred Voss

---

contemporary crafts inspirational gifts

cusp

28 Back Swinegate   York   YO1 8AD   Tel/fax: 01904 622400

THEY COULD HAVE HAD PHDS TOO

I have seen men
on grinding wheels who could hum
a movement from Beethoven's 5th note for note quote
Gandhi
Walt Whitman I have seen men
with welding rods in their hands with hearts
closer to Jesus
than any professor in any office men
who truly know what it means to walk out of a factory after 40 hours
without one drop of blood
on their hands one fired
man on their conscience one false
smile or word on their lips men
who stand at their machines handling parts all day with the dream
they had when they were 4
still somehow
in their hearts men freer
with brass dust all over their hands than presidents
or kings will ever be men
who can look at themeselves in the mirror and laugh
like the wisest man
who ever lived even though
they never finished 8th grade men
too fine
to need medals on chests or degrees on walls or gold-plated
Cadillacs men
who have the music that makes the galaxies
shine
in their fingers tapping the top of a sheet metal workbench
with joy.

Fred Voss

MOVING INTO OUR NEW HOME

Once a year when the factory owner takes the supervisors and half the workers
on that fishing trip off the Santa Barbara coast
we machinists and de-burrers and part-packers left
turn up
our radios extra loud and listen to mariachi
or jazz or heavy metal music
like we would at home.
Some go to drinking fountains with coffee mugs
and fill the mugs with water and spend as much time
as they like watering the potted
green plants they keep beside their machines
or grinding wheels
some
stop what they are doing to gaze
whenever they feel like it at photos
of children and grandchildren they take out of their wallets
and prop
against pans full of finished brass or steel parts
as others
of us wander about the shop getting to know each other
a little bit while our machines
run or
go up to each other and say,
'Got it done yet?'
like the supervisor is always doing
and laugh hysterically at our imitations of him
as we hold our heads high
and look around at the tin walls
like we really live there
and everywhere
in this shop men and women in work aprons and steel-toed shoes
begin to smile
like they are human.

Fred Voss

Calls from Home

I feel settled here, five thousand miles away,
and yet each night dreams suck me back
across the Atlantic, rewinding four decades
in the blink of an eye.

See down our garden, over the bank,
where the Welland flows in slow-motion
in that twilight time of secret games —
My sisters and brother call out
from their hiding places in the dock-leaf jungle
and I unravel like a spinning-top
on the pear tree swing.

Mum's shape appears in the lighted doorway
calling us in — down the stone step
and into the old house (not yet demolished) —
where every beam, latch and flagstone
is back in its place,

and Dad is alive, sitting in his armchair,
ready to rub our hair dry by the fire.

Marion Ashton

BREAK

At a certain point the work becomes enough
A book's weight grows dense like a weary head
I place it, closed and smoothed, on the desk
and let the pen roll from my fingers
to settle on a near filled page,
strands of thought I can resume again
Library lamps nod, muted green, when I pass

Words subside as I cross a damp street home
past hushed shadow gardens and latched gates
Steady lights press against blocks of glass,
reminding my mind to warm and dissolve
If I met a stranger I could take her palm,
rest it on my heart to share its hidden pulse,
a subdued constant rushing that pushes low and soft
like a determined, patient, guiding stream

Natalie Ford

Mr ISBN

Travelling in the Midwest a few years ago I came across the case of a man who changed his name. This in itself is nothing noteworthy these days: film stars and musicians, after all, do it all the time, as do those tired of their given names, and many who are plain eccentric. In the latter category, for instance, I would include Haywood Ritter of Indiana, who in 1989 became Chicken Chicken Jones. I recall, also, a joke told me by a friend from New York about Joe Horsepiss who asked the judge to change his name from Joe to Dan, but that's another story and not funny to me now I'm no longer a 20-year old pot-smoker.

What intrigued me about Paul E Stankovitch was that he became Mr ISBN 187477840X: surely the first case of a man who voluntarily became a number. For those of you unaware of this form of code - an ISBN (which stands for Intternational Standard Book Number) is the unique number which identifies a particular edition of a book. After the change Stankovitch insisted on the 'Mr' part, by the way.

Unfortunately I didn't keep the article from the paper where I read about this transformation, on account of being in a hurry and having other matters on my mind at the time. I did, however, and for some reason which I cannot remember, write down the actual number. The only other detail I can recall from the article was that Mr ISBN 187477840X worked for a local utility company who had not looked upon his self-appointed name-change with pleasure. Neither had the Inland Revenue Service at first. He also had a dog called Nixon, but he wasn't planning to change his name. It occurred to me that if the dog was one of a long line of hounds he could give his an ISSN - an International Standard Serial Number, like a magazine.

I occasionally thought about Mr ISBN 187477840X. What did his friends and family call him, for instance? Was he called 'Is' or 'Isbn'? Or 'Ice'? Did some of his workmates call him '40X'? Did ISBN serve as a first name at all? It wouldn't be a problem to his kids, if he had any. He'd just be plain 'dad' or 'pop'. But I can't imagine his mother or father calling him anything but Paul. Can you?

If he was an embarrassment to his friends and family, they must be used to it by now. He's only a mystery to people who don't know him, like me. Why a book? Why not a title of a book instead of its number? Did he read too many books? Was he a local genius with no outlet for his creativity? Was he a homegrown Thoreau making a statement? Was he mad? Did he do it for a bet? Sometimes I muse on these things while I'm sat on a plane over Utah or the Atlantic.

I checked out the number on various databases and no book exists that fits. So he is unique. Maybe he *is* the book he's writing so he is literally writing his own life. I like to think that's the case. At least, that's what I think on Thursdays.

Michael Blackburn

THE BIG FIGHT

In the right corner!
In ever green trunks!
Weighing 185 trees!
Looking fit to drop
a few cliches in the clinches!
From Hand-Me-Down-Land!
The Undisputed Champion!
Old Man An-thology!

In the wrong corner!
In candy striped trunks!
Weighing 500 small presses!
In all kind of shapes.
From Hard Edge, Graffiti,
Pencil-maia!
The Challenger!
Joe (Performance) Po-etry!

Your Referee for the Evening
ladies and gentlemen,
The one and only! —
Roget's Thesaurus!
Your Judges, as always,
Passion Fashion and Posterity!

*   *   *   *   *

Now, I want a good clean fight.
No back-biting or swearing.
No snarling rapping or ranting.
No spitting or psyching.
No splitting infinitives.
And no going for the lowlands.
Now, shake hands and...

Wait for the bell you crazy bastards!

Dave Mason

THE HOLE   Came hollowing through space,
limbering up to become something
more than a ring of nothing,
weary of being pushed around

by vibration and neutrinos
of little substance, zero tolerance.
It sought a vacant amorphous place,
somewhere that disliked density.

Then an area found it to be
an opening, a means to an end.
It flourished, spread, diversified,
got in shape, learnt to circulate.

Soon it was putting on airs,
making its absence felt everywhere,
absorbing corners, nooks and crannys,
planning wholesale take-over bids.

It holed up near the Grand Canyon,
appeared on an explorer's website
showings its own holistic logo -
'You'll Never Hold A Good Hole Down.'

Slowly it grew too big for its role,
was identified as a gaping chasm,
refused to be taxed by specific gravity,
so unwholesome forces filled it in.

That's the hole story.

Dave Mason

THAT LAST HELLO

The Sparrow shall hop and sing at dawn. Dawn the smudge of light found bleeding in the gaps in Crow's wing. Criss-crossed shards of frost pricking the morning and Sparrow shall strut behind the narrow barrel of his chest. Hair, those strands, fine wires of gray and brown again to be re-raked across the baby pink shell of Sparrow's skull.

In Sparrow's pocket a gnawed rabbit's foot for luck, a withered rake of white heather for extra-luck and a black rat's severed head for farewell - the only trinity he's ever needing. Crow had found the rat snaking between fat yellow fingers of bananas. Crow had laughed. Huge blocks of ice teeth biting a smile out of empty air. The chase was slow: move, rat, move, living yellow ripple of banana, sedulous pursuit of long piano fingers. In the dusty corner of the banana box the rat turned. Six inches of indignant fury arched with hate. Lurch, rat, lurch, and high in the air black rat springs into the silent curve of steady fingers: gripping, gripping - feel throb of heartbeat.

'What you got there, Crow?'

Crow turned to laugh at Sparrow. Crow is the child. Huge, raw boned strong Crow with the mind of a child. 'Hello,' replied the Crow.

'Hello' drips in fat vowels and heavy Ls while the huh is breathed with the whole of his chest. Only once did 'hello' sound different, that time the Sparrow found Crow late one night, when men had prised the Crow from his shelter behind empty market crates. They had dragged out Crow taking it in turns to hurt him. Sparrow found Crow in a sticky pool of velvet. Under the weak flame of Sparrow's guttering lighter, Crow's blood showed flame red, and from the broken mouth came, 'Hello' in thick clots of wounded sound.

Sparrow had spat on his discoloured hanky and wiped in light stroking dabs the gore from his friend's face. Crow hadn't cried, perhaps he didn't have the mind of a child.

Crow had cried when he felt little heart stop. Black rat died through fright. Black rat was held one-handed all that morning. Crow the giant worked the market, heaving great caskets of fruit with one hand. Crow felt his own heart bursting. Crow felt his great strength falter, but one hand was for dead heart of the rat. Next day in his top dungaree pocket rat lay within the wrinkled bedding of torn banana-leaf.

When rat's body bloated with death, Sparrow pecked off his head with penknife. Death with luck sits in one pocket of the Sparrow.

Dawn, pale dawn purple tinged with winter or hot angry bursting orange dawn of summer, Sparrow shall check his pocketed totems afore scratting for breakfast. Each and every morning while Crow, head thrown back, snores those welling volcano-roars that rupture daybreak, Sparrow preens his sparse scalp and totters to the sandwich-wagon. In his inside pocket battered sheaves of notes are uncurled for breakfast. Sparrow skips back to Crow his thin arms laden. Small spiteful bitefuls of bacon sandwich Sparrow takes, all the while his ankle kicks the open spreading belly of Crow.

'Hello' will say Crow and the kicking stops and a playful smile spreads thin on Sparrow's lips and Crow laughs taking his two sandwiches.

The market is alive now with vans and trucks. Sparrow struts directing traffic, allotting stalls while piping at the top of his thin reed voice. The Crow lumbers from van to van from truck to truck, loading, unloading and swinging his scaffold-key he starts to right, extend, strip and rebuild temporary stalls. Everyone likes Crow. His slow quiet strength, his warm rumbling 'hello'.

Sparrow is the one to watch.

Crow watches Sparrow. He wishes he were Sparrow. Men move for Sparrow.

Sparrow says this, Sparrow says that and all jump and move for Sparrow. Men give Sparrow money. Men give Crow scraps of food and clothing. Sparrow is good to Crow, but he wished he was the Sparrow, then Crow could sit and smoke most of the day.

Most of the day Crow shall sweat. Most of the day Crow shall thirst. Throughout the day Crow slaves still smiling 'hello'.

Folk pity poor Crow.

'You treat the Crow wrong, Sparrow,' said a man. 'I don't treat my burro half ways as bad.'

'Your burro ain't as strong as Crow.'

'Sparrow what you saying, you got less sense than Cripple Crow.' Excited, hot fast eyes, sharp piping call, 'Crow, here, Crow!'

And the Crow came. The sun a blister of yellow spiked in the sky. Men and women and street children milling while Sparrow talked up the bet, pulling a tardy flat cap from his pocket, stakes placed and the bet made.

'Go, Crow, go, Crow, go Crow, go,' shrieked the Sparrow, dancing up and down the line of the tug of war atween Crow and the burro. Ropes pull and cut dark Crow-flesh. Strange whinnies break and snort from the burro - 'Go, Crow, go,' hops the Sparrow and Crow's huge thick lips rip into unknown scowls and the burro slides on cracked hoofs - 'Go, Crow, go.' And the Sparrow dances on spindle pegs of legs and the Burro is whipped by the man, but Crow is on all fours inching his way forward in bruised gasps of breath - 'Go, Crow, go,' sings the Sparrow. Men and women and street children cheer, but the burro has collapsed still whipped by the man as Crow pulls and snorts like a bull, ploughing the dried mud ruts of Market Street.

Crow cried when he saw the Burro. Blood, mucus and hot hum of fly crowd Burro's nose. Crow thought that his heart would break. Crow hung his head, tucked in his knees spending the day behind banana crates' shade. Sparrow's cap was full. He smoked and passed around the best white rum.

No one pitied poor Crow.

Sparrow felt angry with Crow. Sparrow was drunk. He wanted to get Crow drunk. When Crow drunk, he laugh and dance. Crow was sulking. How could Crow sulk when he, Sparrow, had won much money for them that day: stupid peasant and broken burro. Sparrow hunted for Crow. He found him alone in the purple blackness. He wasn't sleeping, but his breath came laboured. Sparrow's blue bead eyes misted over. Sparrow walked from Market Street to corner stall, by the quay there he bought a cracked bowl of goat curry. Sparrow left the bowl by Crow. Crow mumbled 'Hello' and tried to eat. The food tasted like mud in the rainy season. The food tasted like street-dust in the dry season. Crow spat the food from his mouth - 'Go, Crow, eat, Crow,' said Sparrow.

Before the food became cold and swam with flies, Sparrow ate, leaving nothing. His short pink tongue and grubby white fingers cleaned the broken bowl for scraps of food.

Sparrow walked back to food-shop corner. Crow will eat in the morning. Crow likes huge bacon sandwiches with hot chili sauce. Crow will work in the sun tomorrow, perhaps another peasant Indian shall come to wager a burro. Sparrow returned the cracked bowl, drank white rum and kissed the hand of the red girl afore limping back to Market Street.

Sun sets quickly. Sparrow crouches under cold-cold Crow's wing. Night hides Market Street. Sparrow rocks holding his knees atween thin fleshless fingers. He would cry, but for the black rat head held in his mouth.

Crow kiant say hello no more.

Daithidh MacEochaidh

THE MORNING BRINGS

puking in the back seat of a taxi
Richard 'Smitty' Smith
area branch manager
of Eagle Tools
        The Finest in American Craftsmanship
        Made in Dongguan but what the hell
gimmes to the cabbie:
A tissue.
No, not that.
Don't you know?
A TISSUE FOR CHRISSAKE.

Mr Smith seldom bothers with Cantonese
even though he mastered the beginner's course
twice
he says the words alright
he understands himself alright
so what the hell is everyone's problem?

7 years
3 months
14 days
Here a Lan Kwai Fong liver
There a Wan Chai
and now
with orders from the head office in Kansas City
how Mr Smitty Smith will hoot and howl
tomorrow at Chek Lap Kok
when he boards that plane
for home
Home goddammit
the U.S. of fucking A.
where everyone speaks English good
where he'll never have to ride another rickshaw
ask an organ grinder monkey for

ANOTHER TISSUE FOR CHRISSAKE.

Driver Wong strolls around his idling cab
yawns
stretches
parks his elbow on the hood
readies himself for a cigarette

hell of a mess getting that *gweilo* home
he'll clean up the back seat later
right now Driver Wong wants to savour
the last of his Marlboros
and the first of the sun
beautiful how it stirs the city
how it sobers up neon
into calling it a day.

Driver Wong recalls a story he once heard
a Western story
about a foolish man
who made wings of wax
flew too near the sun
then fell
Driver Wong couldn't remember
how far the foolish man had flown
nor where he had landed

could he have been the one
last night
slumping and sinking
flailing and wailing
lost in the back seat
of his cab?

Timothy Kaiser

GLOSSARY OF MAORI AND NEW ZEALAND ENGLISH USAGE

Te Ao Marama - literally the world of life and light, the world we live in where we should progress to our best selves

kowhai - literally, yellow, pronounced cofe-eye) and the name of the national flower of New Zealand.

'tihei mauriora' - literally, 'the sneeze of life'; metaphorically Behold! I live! - a formal expression used to announce that someone wishes to speak, ceremonial usage

taniwha *(incidentally wh is always pronounced 'ph', and all separate syllables are pronounced individually, i.e. tan-ee-phar)* - a water monster, or ogre, who can also be your guardian spirit, also a being of repute, to be respected

kaumatua - old man, elder, or to become an adult

kutai - mussel

tinana - body (human or e.g. chassis of car), also yourself

kina - sea-egg, sea-urchin

Ngapuhi *(ng is pronounced like the ending - ing, you have to be Maori to get it right, I think - then ar-poo-hee)* - the largest Maori tribe on the North Island - the Treaty Ngapuhi was the Treaty negotiated with that tribe only, which was superseded by the Treaty of Waitangi (1840) the formal alliance under which Maori and Pakeha still live together - very important in New Zealand history

mihi - literally, greeting, also used to designate formal speech-making

Te Reo - the Maori language (literally, our tongue)

aroha - love, sympathy, pity - often used as a girl's name

hui - gathering, meeting, often for discussion where consensus is sought

hongi - Maori traditional greeting, where noses are rubbed - nowadays a very controlled salute!

tangi - a wail, or cry of mourning, and also birdsong

ti - another name for the cabbage tree, which some think should be the national tree of New Zealand rather than the pohutekawa tree ('crimson flower' tree)

kumara - sweet potato and used in many Maori dishes - yummy

paua shell - from the shellfish haliotis - blue-green iridescent and used in much Maori artwork and to decorate wood and bone carvings as well as separately for jewellery

crib and **smoko** are NZ slang

crib, or **bach** is the term used (crib S. Island, bach N. Island) for a holiday home, on the beach, or a shanty for e.g. shepherd up in the hills

smoko is a break for a cigarette (or ciggy) - as in the UK, now taken by workers huddled outside the place of employment, once a sacred perk!

Compiled by Jenny Argante

SOURCES FOR INFORMATION ON NEW ZEALAND WRITERS

The best website to find information about NZ writers is www.bookcouncil.org.nz/writers - the following are there:
www.bookcouncil.org.nz/writers/pireiemark.htm
www.bookcouncil.org.nz/writers/tuwharehone.htm
www.bookcouncil.org.nz/writers/smitherelizabeth
ww.bookcouncil.org.nz/writers/mcqueencilla.htm

REVIEWS

The Tip of My Tongue: Robert Crawford (Cape 2003) 51pp. £8

Scottish poet and academic Crawford is flying high. At St Andrews University, where he is Professor of Modern Scottish Literature, he also presides over the Poetry House, one of the largest poetry centres in the UK. He has a growing publications list – editing jobs, literary titles, plus four volumes of poetry, the last of which, *Spirit Machines*, (1999 Cape) garnered him extravagant praise. The lynch pin of this collection was a twelve page, 360 line meditation on the artist and domestic struggles of C19th Scottish novelist Margaret Oliphant. It's a fiercely cerebral, yet visceral piece, dealing with exile, struggle, the creative imagination and Scottishness – vital themes to any Celt.

So does the new collection cement his reputation as a vigorous, cutting edge voice, assured and individual? Well, oddly, no. This feels like a poet marking time, or perhaps even retreating into what he describes in 'A Scottish Poet' as 'one long/sabbatical from real life.' No harm in that: exploration is the key to development. But a volume so devoted to celebration, after a volume so tied to explorations of sickness and loss, inevitably sacrifices some tension. It's unfortunate too that this spring, though the sunniest on record in Britain, is defined by war. It isn't the best time for paeans of praise to the planet.

There are pleasant love poems, translations from the Latin, and neat evocations of place. Scotland may be the jumping-off point, but there is a clear determination to embrace the world. Not all the poems take advantage of Scots idiom, though the best benefit from an easy movement between standard English and vigorous demotic. Crawford says he uses Scots as a painter uses impasto – to thicken and deepen texture – and this certainly works.

The clue to the collection lies in the dedication – to his wife and children, with love – and to the tag-line – from James Hogg, the C19th Scottish writer, best known for his extraordinary cry of pain *Confessions of a Justified Sinner*. But this quote isn't about Calvinist doom. On the contrary, it suggests that Crawford positions Hogg, and himself, as Romantics committed to investigating 'not the theory of dreams but the dreams themselves'. The words 'I love…' recur, on page after page.

Do we accept the poet's own words about his intentions? He told Isabel Hilton in a Radio 3 interview, 'it's a reaction against my previous book, which was about death, terminals, computing…I want a sense of the future, moving on, a reconnection with the world , such as you have after bereavement…and I try to give a sense of the ways in which Scotland is connected to the wider world too.' So Crawford celebrates marital commitment - 'I love the bigamy of it, the fling/of marriage on top of marriage.'

He marvels at the insouciance of his daughter 'I love how you yell a pirouette…Wee ballerina, pas – de – bas – ing in front of Mons Meg./ Singing down the barrel of that gun.' He celebrates the business of writing 'I love it, the mouth music's make and break/Between lines…' He nods at other Scots poets – Crichton Smith , MacDiarmid, Muir. He has poems in praise of Aberdeen,('I love your hard core') St Andrews ('I love how it comes right out of the blue…') Arbuthnott ('I love the North East…').

The stiff translations, from a little known but much travelled Aberdeenshire poet and scholar, Arthur Johnston, give respect to the North East, whose glens 'Dazzle with gemstones…' to Glasgow: - 'you are a star…' to St Andrews - (yes, again! Has he been nobbled by the local Tourist Board? Perhaps not, but the image of 'hungover students' who 'sober up with golf clubs' leads lesser mortals like this reviewer to picture that University's most famous, and photogenic student, Prince William, practising his swing – fatal bathos!)
Onwards and upwards! In Planetist, he tells us – you guessed – he loves

> all windy grand designs…with my lanky body I thee worship
> Scotland, New Zealand, all national dots,
> The salt of the earth, the pepper of the earth.

How much higher can we go? How much more celebration can we take? 'Acceptance Speech' thanks the planet 'for your gift of tongues'. Finally, in 'From The Top', godlike, 'feet in the clouds' Crawford sees how 'Dutch fields are Berber rugs in a bazaar'. From this Olympian height, Scotland and the world mingle all connected, in a Whitmanesque, Hopkins like vision of unity, beauty and purpose.

> I watch
> Shackleton's shadow cross the Southern Lights
> And swallows brushing Arabic on air…
>
> All things improbable, as God's my witness,
> Barmiyan Buddhas, Easter Island heads,
>
> And everything I see here from the top
> Is overlooked by bens and glens of stars.

Ecstatic, hopeful lines. Small wonder John Muir, early ecologist, traveller and nature writer, is a hero, 'hitched to the universe.' Crawford may be having his universe moment, in this collection, his Laurentian 'Look, we have come through' phase, and who would deny him the right to be happy? The fact is, though, that the most achieved poems combine acute observation with detatchment and distance. The eye is cool, the critical intelligence surgical. The 'Auld Enemy' is a devastating, clever, waspish snipe at the Scottish talent for self – destruction,

> wait till ye smell
> Through coorse dauntless, distilled Jock courage
> The wee trickling smell of their underdog-on-the-make
> fear...

This is good strong stuff, as is the perfectly pitched, elegantly controlled California road poem 'Double Helix', in which

> Licking her pinkie
> One driver watches columns of water. Stars
> Come out of nowhere, like steps in the Okanagan...

There is enough relish for life and all it offers – good and bad, sweet and sour - in these lines. Praise poems are all very well, but, as Crawford says in 'Prayer of Allegiance'

> Oh God, give me a dangerous pair of hands,

That's what poets need to have, in this world. The next volume will confirm whether Robert Crawford's knuckles are soft or skinned.

Reveiwed by Morag McGill

Familiar Possessions: Elizabeth Stott (Northern Lights 2002) 60 pp. paperback £3

One of the things I unashamedly enjoy about train journeys, apart from the time to read a good book, is the opportunity to peep into the back gardens of people's houses, the backyards of factories and stare at the 'ripped backsides' of cities and towns. As the train speeds by, you catch that tantalising glimpse of broken toys, rusting machinery, faded washing and the other sad detritus of our little lives carefully hidden behind the respectable facades of manicured lawns and weedless flowerbeds.

This delightful début collection of short stories is just such a glimpse into those hidden backyards. Elizabeth Stott takes her readers from a damp October garden in England to the flyblown heat of the Middle East and through the windows of her stories we glimpse fragments of individual and isolated lives from a cat-hating spinster, to the debonair and randy widower and from a neglected Naval wife and to the permanently embarrassed adolescent girl.

Although the characters and settings are so different, the intriguing theme threaded through the stories is 'possessions' - cracked, faded and broken, the characters nevertheless cling to them, unwilling to throw them away. Yet curiously they are not items chosen by the characters themselves, but objects that have been imposed upon them by others, objects inherited from dead relatives, or furnishings belonging to the army. There is an ancient Jewish superstition that the dybbuks of dead can enter and possess the living through the possessions of the departed and this is happening for each of the characters. Each character is in different sense possessed by the shades of both the living and the dead, which slowly fossilise the spirit. An incident in opening story 'The Rhododendron Canopy' could be taken as a metaphor for the book's characters.

> She removes the small body of the mouse with a shovel and places it under the dark, sterile canopy of a rhododendron ponticum at the back of her garden. There are other small bundles here, desiccated clumps of feather, skin and bone.

The stories are richly embroidered with detail without losing pace and the writer can conjure a sense of place so effectively that I found myself shivering in the autumn mizzle as 'small bronze leaves collect around the tussocks like confetti' and cottage doors 'swell with the damp'. In the dust of Bahrain 'fine threads of tiny ants run through the rotting food' and the heat is so intense that a 'glass of cold orange squash drips with condensation.' I found myself lingering over some of descriptions, just for the pleasure of sucking the words to make them last.

In the best traditions of classic short stories these deceptively gentle tales continue to haunt and unsettle the mind long after you've closed the book. They make you look anew at the possessions around you, the rusty objects in the corner of your own back garden and broken toys in the attic and ask yourself the chilling question - what is there in your life that you really chose for yourself?

Reviewed by Karen Maitland

Festival Of Angels: Magdalena Sikking Chávez (ENDpapers 2002) 397pp. paperback

Do you ever get those weeks where certain themes keep smacking you round the face and you're not quite sure what someone up there is trying to tell you. In my case, I keep tripping over angels - first Simon Armitage's melting snow angel, then Brian Patten's fallen angel 'bleeding among the winter marigolds,' now this unusual novel *Festival of Angels*.

It was written to raise money for the Neighbourhood Association in The Quarter in York who each year before Christmas hold a Festival of Angels to bring tourists and shoppers into the district. Numerous organisations try to raise money through books, but few, if any, are imaginative enough to do it through a novel.

This is a contemporary story set in The Quarter in York amongst the multi-ethnic bars and shops. The plot revolves around drug trafficking, corrupt police and a child who goes missing during the Festival of Angels. The main characters initially appear flamboyant and bohemian, attempting a modern version of the Parisian left-bank lifestyle, but getting their wings regularly clipped by the mundane of modern life - rubbish collection disputes, drinks licensing laws and those backside-numbing community committee meetings we've all had to endure at sometime in our lives. I have to confess I took a malicious pleasure in those scenes, recognising all the character-types from nightmare-committees-I-have-known. Is there a prayer that begins St. Michael and all angels defends us from the perils of committee meetings? If not, there should be.

Interwoven throughout the main narrative, written in 'Realtime', are poetic, almost surreal passages written in 'Angeltime', some just a single line - Of what is the spirit made? Hovering in the Angeltime pieces are the musings of the medieval scholar Alcuin, subtly reminding us that we cannot tread on a flagstone in York without treading on the dreams of ghosts. And ghost-thoughts of the characters also inhabit the Angeltime narration. They are the characters' nobler thoughts, angelically inspired insights that sadly as with all of us, have a tendency to melt like snow angels on contact with Realtime.

There is, perhaps, too much exposition in some of the dialogue, which makes some scenes stilted and slows the pace of the story. Tying a novel so closely to a small place which readers know well can make the author feel that they have to adhere to the facts of geography at the expense of the truth of the story, but in this case the sense that I could actually go to

The Quarters, touch them and smell them, gave me an extra thrill when reading the novel.

In a way the drugs racket is just a sprinkling of angel dust on a story, which is principally about a much deeper issue - the cat's cradle of connections that intricately tangles the lives of the characters together. The inconsequential actions of each person impacts on the lives of those around them creating a sense of community in a modern world, which we are often told has lost its community-feelings. Of what is the spirit made? In this case not of family, religion or ethnicity, but of trust and accident of place. A place to which most have come as modern pilgrims in search of the 'plastic grail.' Perhaps that will be the only spirit that can bind us together in the future.

What I love about this novel is the way that, as for our medieval ancestors, angels and devils, heaven and hell are as much a part of the real world as cabbages and cowpats, so the underworld of drug dealing is spoken of in the same breath as committee meetings and you can almost believe that in The Quarter angels do lean on wheelie-bins and watch the tourists go by. And just in case you should forget why this novel was written, inside the book is little bookmark in the form of a metal ice-angel. OK. OK I've got the hint - I promise I'll go to the Festival of Angels this year.

Reviewed by Karen Maitland

Kavita T.F.Griffin: (Shoestring Press 2003) 55pp. £6.50

While it's unusual to begin with reference to the cover of the book under review, in this case Dan Lyon's beautifully intense design (a vivid close up of a red rose) is an excellent place to start. What on the surface appears to be a conventional, almost sentimental image is in fact an invitation for us to look long and hard at something grown hackneyed through familiarity. The process of looking forces us to see the thing afresh, with all its potential and imperfection. This is what T.F. Griffin's poetry does. Add to that the positively Blakean significance of the symbol of the rose and you have, encapsulated in this single image, much of what Griffin's poetry has come to be 'about'. The publication of this long-awaited collection (*Cider Days* appeared in 1990) confirms Griffin's status as a major talent - a unique voice crying in the wilderness of contemporary poetry.

A review of this length can do little to cover the range and depth that's manifested here; the political and philosophical agenda, the sharp-edged lyrics that imprint themselves firmly in the mind's eye of the reader. What I'd like to do, however, is to draw attention to the shift that has occurred between these two collections. the poems in *Kavita* have a human dimension, shot through as they are with compassion and anger. The whole collection circulates around a core of three elegies - the title poem, 'For Mary Cann' and 'For Tony Earnshaw' where Griffin remembers the life of his artist friend, lived at odds with the 'rule makers' of this commercially driven world who 'Smirk behind the glass/ of their unrecorded greed'. It is as if, by contemplating mortality, Griffin releases the best of his gifts: a spare, uncompromising vocabulary, an impassioned sensibility and an acute ear for the rhythms of the speaking voice pushed to its limits by rage and grief. It is the sort of poetry Keith Douglas might have written had he survived the war he wrote about.

Griffin has come a long way since his first appearance along with other Hull poets in the Douglas Dunn anthology *A Rumoured City*. In many ways he's come to resemble the 'unacknowledged legislator' of his own powerful elegy for the artist Tony Earnshaw and of Shelley's persuasive argument for the enduring sigificance of poetry; and, in the process, taking his readers on a difficult, faltering, but ultimately transforming journey towards the light. Beginning with the possibility of 'love extinquished' Griffin has moved to a position where love itself has become the transforming agent in human affairs. Comparison of his two major collections make this clear: in *Cider Days* he invented a city; in Kavita he's begun to explore it.

Reviewed by Ian Parks

Selected Poems: Razmik Davoyan, translated by Armie Tamrazian (McMillan Publishing Limited 2002) 116 pp. Price unknown

It is always interesting to find a poet new to you who arrives fully formed. This is so with the collection by an Armenian poet who has published 20 collections in his own country that have been widely translated into Eastern European languages but not previously into English. This collection draws on a number of past publications, though sadly the book is light on detail beyond the poems themselves.

I have always enjoyed European poetry despite the fact that I must usually read it in translation. While British poetry of late seems to be veering back towards the stodgily erudite and though American poetry is great on experimentation and introspection, the Europeans generally use their extensive histories and political experiences to develop a poetry which is both broad and gives a sense of place and time, purpose and person. And Armenia has had a long history that is far from over, despite being freed some time ago from the prison that was the Soviet Union.

The European poet does not let us down. As an advisory to the current President of Armenian we can assume that politics and history loom large in Razmik Davoyan's life. His brief introduction concludes that writers write because they are unable not to write, and that writing is a form of creativity that passes the essence of life from writer to reader.

Even a brief acquaintance with recent Eastern European history lends significance to his poem 'The Spider' with its assertion that:

> Not even making a sound,
> Concentrating hard.
> Our sleepless friends,
> Concentrating friends
> Weave webs for our minds
> Every hour of every day.
>
> Moving their thin, fragile legs,
> Soft as darkness crushed in the fist,
> Deformed as darkness in the fist,
> They walk through the night
> In silence....

Whilst some of the phrases which creep into the poems are a little flowery from time to time this may well be a matter of form in Amenian poetry. But the images are strong as in 'And Return'.

> The breezes have found
> Some gossip tonight
> And are throwing it to each other

or in 'The Lamp'

> Pavements, your chests are aching.
> Your bodies are shattered
> then patched up again,
> And your hearts which hide deep within
> Keep sighing from that unknown depth.
> And pavements, Your chests are aching terribly,
> I can feel the pain through my feet.

There is a deeper philosophy underlying these poems than in many other collections. In 'My Twisted Songs' the poet writes:

> I have entered a rock
> Hollowed by the strength of my voice
> And I grind golden grains of patience
> With the millstones of history.

It is this deeper thought and provocation that sets this book apart from a number of others and establishes an agenda for struggle and strength and truth.

Whilst I enjoyed the book I have a quibble with the editor allowing some of the punctuation to go apparently unchallenged. It is used needlessly at times and gets in the way of reading the poems. Whether it makes better sense in Armenian or whether the translator is uncertain of the best uses of punctuation in English I don't know but sound editing should have helped to consider this issue.

Clearly Razmik Davoyan is a great poet in his own land and his voice deserves to be heard in English too.

Reviewed by Nigel Walker

Biographies

ALISTAIR PATERSON, long and respected as a poet, editor, anthologist, writer of fiction, critic and literary judge, is honoured for the quality of his own work and his reliable imaginative editing of *Poetry New Zealand*. It has flourished due to his intellectual and managerial acumen. He's been in the Royal New Zealand Navy and the Police. Paterson is a fierce debater and defender of contemporary poetics and renown for encouraging new talent. He has had seven books of his own poetry published.

ELIZABETH SMITHER has published 12 collections of poems distinctive - not to say idiosyncratic - in the choice of subjects and also in her witty informed style. She has a great feel for the paradoxical in language and is responsive to literary inspiration. Smither was born in New Plymouth where she still works as a librarian.

MARK PIRIE is a Wellington-based poet and publisher with a lively interest in his fellow-writers and in the literature of New Zealand and the world. He has published five collections of poetry, the most recent being *Dumber*, from the Earl of Seacliff Art Workshop.

DENIS WELCH was born and raised on the western plains of Masterton. He always wanted to be a writer, but his ambitions received a setback when, as a boy, he was badly frightened by a split infinitive. He did so poorly at university there was only one career possible for him: journalist. One of T.S. Eliot's greatest fans, and a published poet himself, Welch is world-famous as a *Listener* columnist in New Zealand and freelance writer. *Ordinary Son* was first published April 27th 2002.

HONE TUWHARE is New Zealand's most distinguished Maori poet, a writer of universal appeal, whose poetry is rooted in his peoples' oratory and storytelling traditions. He makes inventive use of New Zealand demotic idioms and deals with age-old themes of lyrical poetry: love, friendship, loss and death - poems of depth and clarity unashamed to be emotional, political and direct.

KAY MCGREGOR is a member of the Rotorua Mad Poets who manage to meet every Monday and write to a theme. She has had poems published in anthologies, and has taken poetry into local schools.

PATRICIA PRIME, lives in Auckland, is a poet and reviewer, with work widely published. She co-edits the New Zealand haiku magazine, *kokako*, is reviews' editor of *Metverse Muse, Poets International, Voice of Kolkata* and Internet magazine *Stylus*.

CATHERINE MAIR, poet and short story writer, recently completed two children's readers series books about special needs children, forthcoming from Gilt Edge Publishing. Instigator of the Katikati Haiku Pathway, featuring international haiku inscribed on boulders. **Patricia Prime** & **Catherine Mair** also write poems together.

TIM UPPERTON is the Customer Services Manager for the Whangarei District Council. He won the Northland Short Story Competition in 2000 (with "The Tent Factory"), and again in 2002. His poems have been published in *Sport, North and South* and *Takahe*, and he was the winner of the Takahe Poetry Competition in 2000.

JAMES NORCLIFFE, fiction editor of *Takahe* magazine, also is a poet of some repute, with a fourth collection just out. A recent Robert Burns fellow at Otago University a prestigious writing fellowships. Published in UK journals including *The Rialto, Stand, Tabla Book of New Verse, Planet, Envoi* and a dozen oe so others.

TIM O'BRIEN is a mental health nurse and part-time writer. He lives in Auckland. Nuclear Free was first published in *Takahe 48*. He has had other stories published in *Words* and *Carve*, and read on National Radio.

MICHAEL LEE has recently left Tauranga where he first began writing poetry for his home town of Nelson. He is a toastmaster and teacher of English.

SUE EMMS, a Tauranga writer, has published short stories, poems and articles in England, USA and New Zealand; and has done well in literary awards in both England and New Zealand. Her first novel, *Parrot Parfait*, was short-listed in the inaugural 2001 Richard Webster Popular Fiction Award, and has just been published to excellent reviews.

PETER FARREL, born in East End, London (1940), arrived in New Zealand (1965). Worked at Waikune Prison, part of conditions for government assisted immigration. In Wellington since the late sixties, he's been a librarian, clerk, policy analyst, Ministerial secretary and a director on the Te Papa Museum project. A Whitireia advanced diploma graduate, he now writes almost fulltime. His work's appeared on Radio New Zealand and has succeeded in local short story competitions.

OWEN BULLOCK, lives in Waihi, Southern Coromandel. He writes songs, haiku, stories and scripts. His first love is contemporary poetry, published in *Poetry NZ, Sport, Spin,* etc, and his haiku have been included in most of the world's leading haiku magazines. He is active in public performances of his poetry and songs.

CILLA MCQUEEN, born in Birmingham (UK) came to New Zealand as a child. She remains committed to the Otago region and to the landscapes of Godzone. For her, poetry emerged from diary jottings, and this is reflected in the rich mixture she offers of casual acquaintances, moments and days, the ordinary seen from unusual perspectives. Much of her work is decorated with her own bold line drawings.

JENNIFER COMPTON is a New Zealander living in Australia. *The Big Picture performed by the Griffin Theatre* (Sydney) & *Cirea* (Wellington) is published by Currency Press; *Blue* a poetry collection (Cinninderra Press) short-listed for the NSW Premier's Prize in 2001.

MANDY COE's collection *Pinning the Tail on the Donkey* (published by Spike, Liverpool) was short-listed for the Aldeburgh Poetry Festival Prize. Her work has been featured on BBC radio and television. Her second collection is to be published by Shoestring Press in 2003.

JILL EULALIE DAWSON (Sudbury, UK), a retired social worker, her poetry has appeared in literary journals in Canada and UK. One book is out: *Deed of Gift*, 1995.

An award-winning poet, playwright CHAR MARCH's latest collection *Deadly Sensitive* is out from Grassroots. Currently she writes for television and is finishing a full length stage play.

DAVID FORD is a senior civil servant in the Home Office. His poetry has been published in magazines and displayed on London buses.

IDRIS CAFFREY from Rhayader in Mid-Wales, lives in Tamworth. A fifth poetry collection, *Departures and Returns* (Peer Poetry International, 2002) is available from 26 Arlinton House, Bath Street, Bath BA1 1QN.

LOTTE KRAMER is a well published poet who appeared in *Passionate Renewal, Jewish Poetry in Britain Since 1945, An Anthology* (Five Leaves, 2001). Latest collection *Phantom Lane* (Rockingham Press, 2000).

UGBANA OYET from Poole UK

MANDY MACFARLANE is from Dundee, Scotland, but is now based in Leeds. She has completed her first collection of short stories and is now working on her first novel.

SAM GARDINER, member of Market Rasen Writers' Group, Louth Poetry Society, won a 2002 Arts Council Writers' Award. In 1994 won the National Poetry competition. Born in Ireland he's lived in Lincolnshire since 1979. His work has recently appeared in *TLS, Arete, Dream Catcher.*

GLORIA GROVES-STEPHENSEN (North Yorkshire) Early, she 'escaped' her hometown in Co Durham and worked as a barmaid in London. Since she's lived in Kenya, Berlin, Cyprus; returning (1961) she trained as an artist. Now she writes whatever she fancies and painst as the mood takes her.

LUCY BRENNAN, born in Dublin, emigrated to Canada in 1957. Her poetry has been well received by Canadian, Irish journals and now a UK magazine. Her collection, *Migrants All* is published by waterShed 1999, Toronto, Canada.

R.J.STALLON, featuring in the 1999 Spotlight Poets series, has had *Survivors - Selected Poems* published (Arrival Press, Peterborough). A new collection of poetry and prose is forthcoming.

ELIZABETH STOTT (Cumbria UK) a physics graduate, has published short stories and poetry in various magazines, with a collection of short stories, *Familiar Possessions*, published by Northern Lights 2002. She is working on a novel.

MARK CZANIK grew up in Hereford and now lives in Bath. Recent poems and stories have appeared in *Other Poetry, Staple, Smiths Knoll, Thumbscrew, Interpreter's House* and BBC Radio 4. He is working on a novel.

ANDRÉ MANGEOT's short stories have been in *London Magazine* and poems in many UK and American publications (incl. *TLS, Daily Express, The Dark Horse, Chiron Review, Pearl* and *Rattapallax*). In 2002 he was a prizewinner in Bridport and Kent & Sussex competitions, with a first collection due from Shoestring Press in 2003. He's a member of Joy of Six (www.joyofsix.co.uk) which recently played in New York venues.

EMMA-JANE ARKADY with a full collection, *Lithium* (Arc) and four pamphlets out has appeared widely in magazines and newspapers: *Leviathan Quarterly, The Independent on Sunday, Rialto, Dream Catcher* and *Railway Quarterly*. Her current passions are: railways, Boodles and architecture.

K.V. SKEVE's work has appeared in Canadian, UK, U.S, Irish and Austrailan publications, most recently *The North, The Journal, Braquemard, The Black Mountain Review* and *Envoi*. Latest book, *Elemental Mind*, (Broken Jaw Press, 1999, Canada) A chapbook *The Arran Design and Other Poems Recently* (Hilton House, UK). A long expat Canadian, he lives and works in smalltown Swanage on the Dorest coast.

KATHRYN DASZKIEWICZ was brought up in Sunderland but now lives and works in Lincolnshire. she was awarded a bursary by East Midlands Arts and was featured in *New Writing* (Shoestring Press 2001). She has had poems in various major magazines. A pamphlet by Glass Head Press is forth-coming.

JENNY SWANN is a freelance writer and art historian. Her work has appeared in *The Spectator, London Magazine, Thumbscrew, Oxford Poetry* and elsewhere. A first full collection *Soft Landing* (2002) and a pamphlet due out from Shoestring in 2003.

GORDON WARDMAN ex-pat Geordie, long resident in Essex. Published novels in 1980s. Since then various poetry collections, latest *Caedmon, the Common Shoddy of the Tongue* (Odyssey)

JULIA DAVIS's visit to Israel in 2000 changed her poetry's nature and form. Since then she's appeared in *Poetry Greece, Brando's Hat, Pennine Platform, Stovepipe* (US) and *Dream Catcher*. She read at the Edinburgh Festival in 2001. Her collection is *Half Asleep Tree* (Belle Vue Press); a new collection's forthcoming from Glass Head Press.

Ruth Beckett: (East Yorkshire) English teacher, grew up on a farm at the foot of the Yorkshire wolds. After a degree in English and History, she read for a MA in Medieval Studies followed by a doctorate in comparative medievalism at the University of York. Her work was first published in *Dream Catcher 6*.

Chris Firth won a 2000 Arts Council Writers' Award. Publications include: *Miasma* (a novel), *The Electroglade Tales*. He's edited *The Unexpected Pond* (Route), *Hullabaloo* (Solomon), *Whitby Stories* & *Witches of North Yorkshire* (Caedom Press) ~~SINAP~~ has published *The Electroglade Tales* this year. (See ad about book.)

Angel Rigby (writer & artist) began writing for publication after her marriage in 1992. Her first poetry collection *The Deep Darkness of Love* came out in 2002, the same year as her first art exhibition.

Mike Barlow is a poet and visual artist living near Lancaster. His work has appeared in magazines and competition anthologies.

Ian Seed has been in print since 1974. From the early 1980s he's worked at various jobs abroad, picking up languages. In 2000 the poetry collection *Stranger* appeared; widely reviewed and praised. *Rescue*, in 2002 and this year a new book is due from Jazz-Claw Press.

Stephen Baker is from Boston, Lincolnshire. He attends creative writing workshops there.

A young writer **Juned Subhan** is an undergraduate at the University of Glasgow. A collection *Blizzard Sparrow* was completed last year. Her poems have appeared in *The Affectionate Punch*, *The Reader*, *Eclipse*, *Poetry Nottingham International*, *Othe Poetry*, *The New Writer* and *Poetry Monthly*. She's working now on her first novel.

Born in Ballymena, Co. Antrim, **Gary Allen**'s latest collection is *Languages* (Flambard / Black Mountain, 2002). He's been anthologied in *Breaking the Skin - 21th Century Irish Poetry* and *The Backyards of Heaven - Poetry from Ireland, Labrador and Newfoundland*.

Joseph Allen from Ballymena, Co. Antrim, has poems in magazines such as *Orbis*, *Billy Liar*, *The Reader*, *Poetry Ireland Review* and *Fortnight*; a pamphlet *Night Patrol* and a first full collection, *Landscaping* (Flambard/Black Mountain, 2003) are due out.

EDWARD STOREY has published seven collections from a variety of poetry presses, plus ten books of non-fiction on Fenland-life, or John Clare, and a biography on the poet and an autobiography. *New and Selected Poems* is just out from Rockingham Press. He has, as the back cover says, 'established a reputation for his individual voice and craftsmanship.'

MARIO PETRUCCI, an experienced poet, writer and Arvon tutor has a PBS recommended collection, *Shrapnel and Sheets* (Headland). Also won major international awards, including London Writers Competition (twice), the Sheffield Thursday (twice) the Bridport and the prestigious Arts Council Writers' Award in 2002. http//mariopetrucci.port5.com

CATHY GRINDROD's poetry has been widely published in magazines and anthologies. Author of one pamphlet she has a full collection, *Fighting Talk*, forthcoming. She works as Literature Officer for Nottingham City and is a poetry workshop and course leader.

IAN PARKS has three collections: *Gargoyles in Winter* (1985), *Sirens* (!991) and *A Climb Through Altered Landscapes* (1998), with monographs on *W.H.Auden: Poems of the 1930s, Robert Graves: The Love Poems* and *Shelley and Revolution* published by the English Assoication. He's won several major awards, the latest from the Royal Literary Fund in 2003. Recent poems in *Poetry Review, The Observer and Poetry* (Chicago).

GORDON WILSON teaches English and Creative Writing at Franklin College, Grimsby. His poems have appeared in *Staple, Poetry Nottingham International* and *Envoi*.

MARY KNIGHT lives in Sheffield and was first published in *Dream Catcher 8*.

INDIA RUSSELL's poetry appears in many magazines with a first collection due next year. She studied music and drama in London, Munich and Bergen. Using her translation she's written and toured a one woman show on Ibsen, *The Secret Room of the Mind*. With musician, Dylan Fowler, premiered her poetry cycle *The Kaleidoscope of Time* at Besminster 2002. She reads her poems widely including at The Troubadour in 2002.

JOHN GREEVES worked at Sussex Unversity then moved to Wales in 1971. He's been published over a range of genres but his main interests are poetry and short stories. His work has appeared in *Fire, Acorn, Anglo-Welsh Poetry Society* and *Borderlines*.

Born in Belfast JAMES CARUTH has lived in South Africa and now lives in Sheffield. He's been published in UK magazines, on the web in the US and broadcast on BBC Radio.

GAIA HOLMES, widely published in magazines (e.g *Brando's Hat, Dream Catcher*) was anthologised in *Poems of Cultural Diversity* (Kala Sagam 1999) and Bradford Library's poet-in-residence in 2000. She seeks a publisher for her first poetry collection.

The Italian **DAVIDE TRAME** lives in Venice and teaches English outside the city. Poems have appeared in *Orbis, South* and *Dream Catcher*; recently in *Poetry Salzburg Review.*

PETER LEWIN has a second collection, *Too Many Winters,* up-coming from Glass Head Press, and *Silverdale* from T.C. Parry Publications, UK. Currently he's working on a long piece about his life in the Lake District for Warwick University Creative Writing Programme.

STUART FLYNN lives in London and first appeared in *Dream Catcher 7.*

ERIN L. HICKEY from Newcastle-upon-Tyne graduates from the University of East Anglia in June 2003. She's had stories and poems in *Acorn* and hopes to start on her first novel soon.

JOOLZ DENBY has four collections (Virgin and Bloodaxe Books); her latest, *Errors of the Spirit* (Flambard). Her novel, *Stone Baby* won the New Crime Writer of the Year Award; her second *Corazon* has been highly praised. A constant poetry performer she has a worldwide following. She lives in Bradford.

FATMA DURMUSH from Turkish Cyprus received 'a sketchy schooling'. Since coming to England she's won the Millennium award for plays and short stories and is published regularly in the *Big Issue.* She has six pamphlets out.

RORY WATERMAN (Lincoln) born in Ireland, grew up mostly in England. He currently studies English at the University of Leicester. Poems have appeared in various magazines.

DIVYA MATHUR, editor of *Odyssey: Stories by Indian Women Abroad,* is a poet with four books: *Sandscript, Antehsalia, Perceptions, September 11th* and a story collection *Akrosh.* Among several positions she holds, she is a founder member of The Asha Foundation, Advisor to the Charwood Arts, and Programme Officer for the Nehru Centre, London.

Born in Hull, **NORMAN JACKSON** is the author of six poetry books and a study on the novels of William Faulkner. Work has appeared in the *New Yorker, The American Scholar, The Reporter Magazine, The Observer* and *The Sunday Times.* A winner in the 1998 Hull Literature Festival. Latest collection *Fieldwalking* is out from Rue Bella.

Nell Farrell, born and grew up in Eastwood, Nottinghamshire, has lived in Hull, France, York and Liverpool, and now in Sheffield. Poems have appeared in *Dream Catcher, Rain dog, Brando's Hat, Staple, Writing Women* and in the anthology *Poetry As A Foreign Language*. A first short collection is due out this year with Rain Dog.

Pamela Lewis (Nottingham, UK) has been widely published and broadcast with two collections out. She has given readings here and abroad. Her works been translated into Greek, French and Chinese.

Fred Voss, dropping out of an UCLA Ph.D. programme in Eng Lit, worked as a Hollywood busboy, then worked in the steel industry while writing novels and then poetry. Factory experience became his theme. His first collection, *Goodstone Aircraft Company* has been called a classic. Further highly praised collections have followed.

Natalie Ford's poems have received recongition in the Buck County Poet Laureate Contest in Pennsylvania U.S.A. (1997, 2002). She attended the University of York (UK) and was published in *Point Shirley*. Now returned to U.S.A.

Marion E. Ashton divides her time between Texas and Woodhall Spa Lincolnshire.

Michael Blackburn, a freelance writer and artist, lives in Lincolnshire. As well as having published and edited *Sunk Island Review* and Press he's had two poetry books published, the latest *The Ascending Boy*. He also now runs *Art Zero*, http://www.artzero.org.uk

J.Morris's poetry and fiction has been published in literary magazines in the UK and US: *Envoi, Other Poetry, Acumen, Staple, Magma* and *Orbis* (UK), *The Southern Review, Missouri Review, Prairie Schooner, Notre Dame Review, Pleiades* and *Five Points* (US). A chapbook, *Pregnant Blue*, is forthcoming from Flarestack (Redditch).

Dave Mason, ex-comic script-writer, with poems in a few magazines and broadcast on Radio Lancashire, claims to write in 'an approriately postmodern mode of confused playful distrustful bewilderment at his own confused playful distrustful bewilderment.'

Daithidh MacEochaidh, educated at Hull, Huddrsfield, York St. John (Philosophy, English and Poetry) is an award winning poet, short story writer and novelist, currently running Skrev Press which concentrates on shorter fiction. (www.skrev-press.com)

The Canadian **Timothy Kaiser** now lives and works in Hong Kong. His writing has been published in China, Canada and the U.S. He's received serveral awards including first prize in the 2003 Canadian Cross-Cultural Short Story Competition. Much of his Hong Kong poetry is inspired by his wife's ancestral Hakka village.

Dream Catcher

Subscriptions To Dream Catcher Magazine

£15.00 (three issues) inc p&p.
Single issue £5.00 plus £1.20 for p&p.

Cheques should be made
payable to Dream Catcher
and sent to:

Editor, Dream Catcher,
7 Fairfield Street,
Lincoln, LN2 5NE
or
Co-ordinator:
Joe Warner
32 Queens Road, Barnetby-le-Wold,
North Lincolnshire, DN38 6JH

Now welcoming Submissions for
Dream Catcher 13